THIS MY COUNTRY

THIS MY COUNTRY
A VIEW OF ARNHEM LAND
Penny Tweedie

COLLINS
SYDNEY/LONDON

Publisher's Note

The spellings of people and places used in this book were based on local tradition and were checked with those used by the Aboriginal Artists' Agency, Sydney.

© Penny Tweedie, 1985

Designed by Pam Brewster
First published 1985 by William Collins Pty Ltd, Sydney
Typeset by Savage Type Pty Ltd, Brisbane
Printed by South China Printing Co, Hong Kong

National Library of Australia
Cataloguing-in-publication data

Tweedie, Penny, 1940–.
This, my country

Bibliography.
ISBN 0 00 216448 5.

[1]. Aborigines, Australian — Northern Territory —
Arnhem Land — Social life and customs.
[2]. Aborigines, Australian — Northern Territory —
Arnhem Land — Pictorial works. I. Title.

994.29'0049915

ACKNOWLEDGEMENTS

This project was made possible by the co-operation of many people in Arnhem Land, and in particular the hospitality of the people of Ramangining and Maningrida. I would like to mention each by name but the recent deaths of several people have placed me in a dilemma; on the one hand I wish to acknowledge the generous assistance of these people who became my friends, but on the other as it is incorrect in Aboriginal law to mention the names of deceased persons I do not wish to offend their families by using their names. On the advice of others, I have chosen to refer to these people throughout the book by reference to their position within the system of social classificiation known in Arnhem Land as the 'skin' system. However, I wish it to be recorded that the following persons helped make this book possible and I hope that this single written acknowledgement to them will not be considered offensive. With the help and guidance of the families of Malangi, Mandarg, Milpurrur, Nandjiwarra Amagula Bungawuy (skin name Bulain), Bininyuwuy (skin name Balang), Boyun (skin name Gamarang), Bulun Bulun, Djoma, Wunawun, Njiminuma, Gurrmanamana and Maralowonga we were able to begin to learn about life in Arnhem Land and the customs and culture of some of its people; an experience which not only gave us an insight into their unique culture but also taught us more about our own. They gave us the opportunity to question and explore and to learn: for this I am profoundly grateful.

Support for the project was encouraged in 1977 when I received a grant from the Arts Council of Great Britain. This was followed in 1978 by the Aboriginal Arts Board investing in the idea of an audio-visual record of bark painting. Finally National Geographic Magazine sponsored the field expenses. The Australian National University granted Clive Scollay and myself a Creative Arts Fellowship to prepare for and work on the material gathered.

We made three trips to Arnhem Land in 1978 and 1979, once in the 'wet' season and twice in the 'dry'. Permission to work as we did was granted on the understanding that we would not be a burden on the communities we visited and therefore we had to be self-sufficient. Camping and food supplies were no real problem but as mobility was essential we became overly dependant on a four-wheel-drive vehicle, the maintenance of which meant, for example, that we had to ship our own supply of petrol in 44-gallon drums to Ramangining and Maningrida. This ultimately consumed most of our funds.

During the wet season when access by vehicle was impossible, Ansett generously contributed to the airfares.

In 1978, while nervously waiting the final okay to enter Arnhem Land, Greg Miles (ranger) and Jane Moore of Cannon Hill in Arnhem Land introduced us to a wealth of ecological and environmental information and helped us to explore some of the spectacular escarpment country and its rich rock paintings.

In August 1978, the elders of the tribal groups across Northern Australia which comprise the Aboriginal Cultural Foundation organized a major festival on Groote Eylandt and allowed us to record it. Throughout our project, the Foundation's staff, Barbara Spencer and Lance Bennett, provided us with a vital communication link between Arnhem Land and the outside world.

At Ramangining the arts and crafts co-ordinators, Peter Yates and Pat Derango, offered us invaluable advice, friendship, Indian curries and care which sustained us through many a difficult, doubting time. Peter also acted as bush surgeon and performed the unenviable task of extracting three prongs of a barramundi lure from my leg with a pair of wire cutters after an over-enthusiastic fishing expedition.

Anthropologists Joe Reecer, Ian Keen, Howard Morphy and Nick Peterson all gave us good advice but it was Dr Diane Bell's enthusiastic and brutal criticism that was my most valuable encouragement.

I would also like to thank Sandy, Denise and Kathy who shared many of the hassles and may still find red dust under their skin!

And in particular, thank you Clive and Ben, without you this experience would not have been the way it was. Extra ordinary.

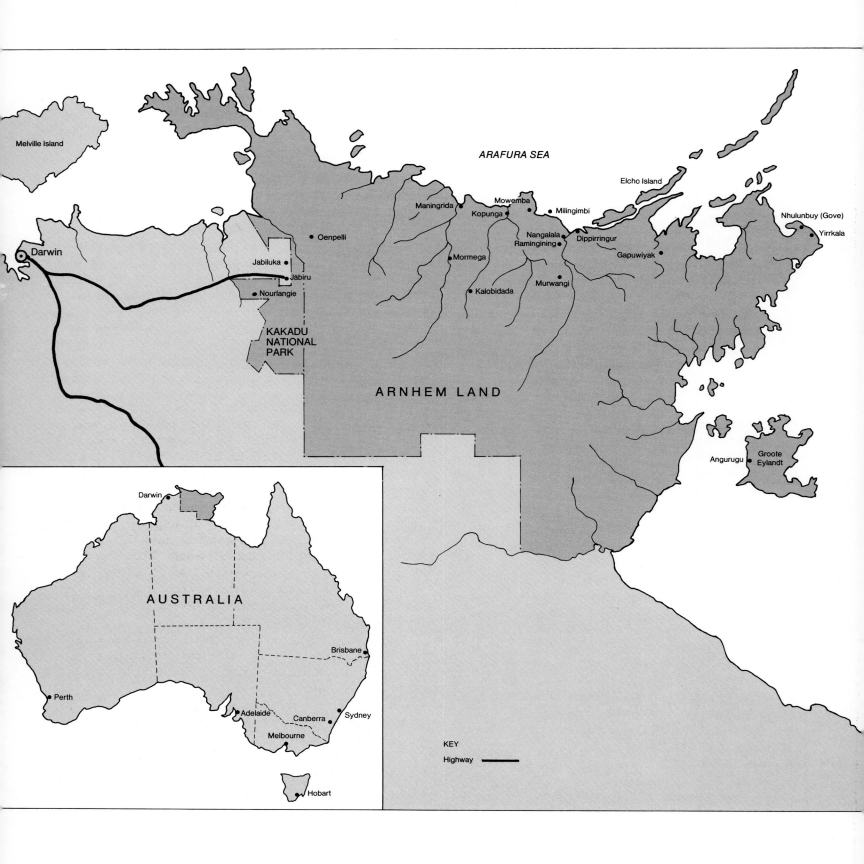

ARAFURA SEA

Melville Island

Maningrida
Mowemba
Kopunga
Milingimbi
Elcho Island
Nhulunbuy (Gove)
Yirrkala
Nangalala
Ramingining
Dippirringur
Oenpelli
Mormega
Gapuwiyak
Darwin
Jabiluka
Jabiru
Murwangi
Kalobidada
Nourlangie

KAKADU
NATIONAL
PARK

ARNHEM LAND

Angurugu
Groote
Eylandt

Darwin

AUSTRALIA

Brisbane

Perth

Adelaide
Canberra
Sydney
Melbourne

Hobart

KEY
Highway

INTRODUCTION

As we have learnt the camera *does* lie. The camera is intrusive, potentially manipulative and exploitative, and never unbiased. Photographs, like words, are always highly subjective and can never portray the entire truth. They can, however, effectively record *moments* of truth.

These photographs, taken in Arnhem Land in 1978 and 1979, cannot be a definitive statement. They are my impression of Aboriginal life, customs and habitat as I experienced them with the help and guidance of many Aboriginal friends. They attempt to present a record of the way of life and customs of some of the Aboriginal people of Arnhem Land, and of a culture that has survived for 40,000 years—a culture now radically threatened by development.

Shortly after arriving in Australia from England in 1975 I became aware of the lack of visual information available to non-Aborigines seeking a better understanding of the original Australians, their unique culture and their continuing struggle for survival and identity. I learnt too, that the proposed mining and development of Arnhem Land posed the greatest threat to the Aborigines and their traditions since the arrival of the first Europeans.

Change is an inevitable part of the business of living, but for the Aborigines of Arnhem Land the present process of change is highly problematical. Many of the concepts involved—land ownership and European law, for example—are alien and the white Australian political system has forced the Aborigines into a position of responding and adapting to change while at the same time refusing them any real control over either the speed or the extent of that change. Contrary to popular belief, Aboriginal culture is not static; but some of the changes now being forced on Aborigines deny them the opportunity to determine and shape their future.

Initial European contact with Terra Australis, the Great Southland as it was known, was made by the Portuguese in 1528. The journals and records of these explorers were lost and the earliest surviving descriptions of the inhabitants of Australia are to be found in Dutch documents dating from 1623.

In that year the Governor of Amboina, present-day Java, commissioned two Dutch vessels, the *Pera* and the *Arnhem*, to explore and chart the Southland. On 18 April 1623 Commander Jan Carstensz recorded his first encounter with the Aborigines on the Gulf of Carpentaria, observing that they were:

Pitch black, thin of body and stark naked, with a twisted basket of net around their head . . . less cunning, bold and evil-natured than the blacks of Nova Guinea, their weapons less deadly.

On 7 May he further noted:

100 blacks tried to prevent us landing . . . some had painted their faces red, and others white.

During their explorations the vessel *Arnhem* under Captain Colster, deserted the *Pera*, taking a course west by northwest for the Dutch East Indies. Colster charted his discoveries which included Groote Eylandt, the Wessel Islands and that part of the northern coast of Australia which was later named *Arnhem Land*, after his ship.

Since the sixteenth century, Indonesian traders, in particular the Macassans, had been visiting the coast of Arnhem Land; Japanese and Asian fishermen had also explored and exploited the coastal waters. The Macassans never settled but visited the northern coast of Arnhem Land to collect trepang—seaslug—a delicacy they traded with the Chinese. Macassan influence on the Aborigines must have been considerable as many songs, stories and dances bear witness to their presence. Macassan fishermen evidently came without their women and many intermarried with Aboriginal women. They introduced alcohol and tobacco and the long smoking pipe that is still used today. Food supplies brought with them included the tamarind, the seeds of which took root around their camps and continue to flourish today. They also introduced the Aborigines to money, the Indonesian word for which, *rupia*, is still used in the Guparpingu language.

More than a century after the *Arnhem* and while the Macassans were still exploiting the northern shores, the

British explorer Captain James Cook landed on the east coast of the continent on 29 April 1770, near what is now Jervis Bay in New South Wales. The following day he attempted to make contact with the Aborigines by offering gifts, but as he recorded in his journal:

. . . about 18 to 20 came on to the beach and made a stand, they would not be enticed by presents nor were they offensive, all they seemed to want was for us to be gone.

George III had commissioned Cook to acquire any uninhabited land for the British Crown or to negotiate a settlement with the indigenous inhabitants. Cook had already expressed his concern for the Aborigines in an official report:

In reality they are far happier than we Europeans . . . they live in tranquillity which is not disturbed by the inequality of condition: the earth and sea furnish them will all things necessary for life . . .

This did not, however, prevent him breaching his commission by raising the Union Jack without consulting the Aborigines. As possession of Aboriginal land or territory did not involve demarcation and thus could not be established in European terms, it was assumed that the natives did not 'own' the land; thus no treaty with the Aborigines was attempted and when in 1788 Governor Phillip and 1,044 men, women and children landed at Sydney Cove to establish the colony of New South Wales, all land was looked on as 'Crown Land'. This mistaken assumption denied the Aborigines any legal title and laid the foundation for the conflict which continues today. Under British law any resistance to this dispossession was an act of treason, punishable by death.

Due to the size and remoteness of the continent it was not until 1824, in response to the threat from French and Dutch territorial interests, that the first settlement in the north was established at Fort Dundas on Melville Island. Instructions from Westminster to the Governor there suggested that he 'promote religion and education among the native inhabitants', but the Aborigines resisted this intrusion by pillaging the early settlements. In 1827 the local authority offered a reward of £5 for any Aborigine alive or dead, thereby exacerbating the situation.

Over the next sixty-five years four further attempts were made to establish a permanent settlement on the north coast, but each was abandoned as a result of tropical disease and conflict with the Aborigines. Finally, in 1869, almost a century after Cook's arrival, a township of tents and log huts was established on the north coast at Port Darwin. Initially named Palmerston after the British Prime Minister of the day, the settlement subsequently became Darwin.

The Northern Territory, covering a million square kilometres—more than ten times the size of England—occupies one sixth of the total landmass of Australia. Its northern part consists of numerous tropical islands and monsoonal lowlands; inland the terrain rises gradually through bush, grassland and semi-desert to the arid desert region in the centre of the continent.

Throughout the nineteenth century explorers and prospectors attempted to conquer this vast wilderness in search of gold and fertile land. Although their expeditions failed to find the 'Eldorado' they anticipated they paved the way for the building of the Overland Telegraph Line in 1872, which connected the Empire's loneliest outpost, Darwin, with the outside world. In the same year the discovery of gold at Pine Creek, south of Darwin, led to a rush that rapidly increased the predominantly male non-Aboriginal population of the Territory. Many of the European settlers, unable to cope with the tropical climate and harsh conditions recruited Chinese immigrants into their labour force. Meanwhile, in London, blocks of land were auctioned to opportunists, some of whom would never set foot in the new colony.

As the settlers pushed further into the hinterland some Aborigines were killed, and others sought refuge with relatives in nearby country. Still others waged guerrilla warfare on the intruders. Of those living near the settled areas some were absorbed into the work force but many were decimated by the introduction of disease, alcohol and opium. Eventually some clans were totally wiped out as these new diseases spread beyond the settled areas.

Epidemics of malaria, smallpox, leprosy and venereal disease dissuaded all but a few European women from venturing north. However, as the European and Asian population increased so too did the exploitation and abduction of Aboriginal women. When the first census was taken for the settlement of Darwin in 1881 it recorded a population of 3,451, of whom 670 were European and 2,781 Chinese or part-Aboriginal. Full-blood Aborigines were not counted.

By the 1880s cattle stations were being established south

of Darwin and the whole of Arnhem Land and was held under eleven pastoral leases. Not only were the Aborigines dispossessed of their land, but the introduction of cattle, sheep and buffalo changed the ecological balance of the country, depriving them of their traditional food sources. Many of the Aborigines, reluctant to leave tribal land to which they had deep spiritual and cultural ties, became slave labour for the pastoralists in return for handouts of tobacco and basic rations—flour, tea, sugar and occasionally offal. Station Aborigines were punished for hunting and prevented from attending ceremonies; their social structure and cultural framework was eroded, their health deteriorated and all too quickly they became dependent upon the white man's handouts.

Those of the Aborigines who had retreated or remained in the bush to continue their semi-nomadic lifestyle were considered by the pastoralists as trespassers in their own country. Conflict escalated. Aborigines stole cattle, were shot by whites, retaliated by spearing stockmen and were massacred by punitive expeditions. The shooting of *myall*—wild Aborigines—became a weekend sport.

Historians have estimated that when the first British settlers arrived in 1788 the continent had an Aboriginal population of at least 300,000. By the end of the nineteenth century poison, disease, genocide and deliberate neglect had reduced this figure to 70,000; white Australia, needing a rationalization for what had happened, had fallen back on the explanation that the Aborigines were a degenerate race of primitives that was destined to die out. However, about this time some of the early explorers began to publish reports and journals of their expeditions. Their interaction with the Aborigines had been varied: some suffered and perished as a result of clashes with the natives, others acclaimed the Aborigines for their skills, beliefs and profound understanding of the land. Edward John Eyre, for example, attributed his success in desert crossings to the help and companionship of the Aborigines. King, the sole survivor of the ill-fated Burke and Wills expedition, was saved from death by a group of Aborigines who fed, clothed and cared for him for nine months.

These reports, and questions from concerned individuals regarding the protection of Aborigines, prompted Christian organizations to set up missions. The Anglican Church Missionary Society established one at Roper River in 1908 and another at Daly River in 1910. At this time, however, the local police were responsible for the control and protection of Aborigines; on their advice the Government of the day decided that all quarter- and half-caste children should be reared as whites and many of them were brutally removed from their Aboriginal mothers and despatched to the mission settlements.

The Commonwealth Government assumed control of the Northern Territory in 1911 and a year later introduced the first Aboriginal Ordinance, under which the Chief Protector, Baldwin Spencer, became the legal guardian of every Aborigine and every part-Aboriginal child. Full-bloods were segregated from half-castes, compounds were set up in Darwin, Alice Springs and Katherine and part-Aboriginal children were again forcibly taken from their families to be placed in institutions. Rigid control of all Aboriginal movement meant the repression of traditional customs and culture; alienated from their land and frequently from their families, Aboriginal people were at the mercy of the oppressor.

Baldwin Spencer, an anthropologist by profession, was appalled by the degradation, disease and discrimination he witnessed and suggested to the Government that care for the Aborigines in the Northern Territory should become a national responsibility. He proposed protection by segregation, with the establishment of large reserves to accommodate full-blood Aborigines. It was a policy of paternalistic apartheid, but at least it recognized some Aboriginal social needs. Spencer's proposal was shelved during the First World War, however, and the debasement of Aboriginal society continued.

During the 1920s several mission settlements were established in Arnhem Land. Milingimbi, set up in 1926, soon came under the supervision of the Rev. T. T. Webb, and was more fortunate than most: Webb had considerable knowledge of Aboriginal culture and his concern influenced mission policy in central and north-east Arnhem Land for several decades.

Pressure on the Government from academics, anthropologists and international organizations to examine the position of Aborigines led to an inquiry headed by J. W. Bleakley in 1928. He produced a plan based on the formation of reserves, calling for segregation, protection, education, training and control. The Government responded in 1931 by proclaiming 95,000 square kilometres of Arnhem Land an Aboriginal reserve and handing the implementation of Bleakley's programme over to the missions. Control of Aborigines tightened: prohibition of alcohol was introduced, segregation of half-castes was extended, racist attitudes hardened and killings and punitive raids continued.

Later reports on Arnhem Land from anthropologists Donald Thomson (1935–36) and Professor A. P. Elkin (1938) forced the Government to reconsider its Aboriginal policy. Thomson criticized the mission institutions and their administrations for being incompatible with Aboriginal culture and nomadic lifestyle and recommended that Arnhem Land be made an inviolable reserve. In 1939 John McEwen, Minister for the Interior, tabled his 'New Deal' for Aborigines in Federal Parliament, the emphasis of which was on assimilation; but again war intervened and no legislation was passed.

During the war, Arnhem Land became the first line of defence against Japanese attack. Darwin suffered repeated air-raids. All white and half-caste women and children were evacuated to the south while many male Aborigines joined the armed forces. By 1944 more than 1,000 Aborigines were employed in the war effort, earning five shillings a week plus full rations, medical care and accommodation. What the 'New Deal' policies of McEwen failed to achieve, the war partially accomplished by accelerating the process of social change. The relatively equal treatment of Aborigines and white Australians led the Aborigines to a new set of expectations which exposed the exploitative attitude of the pastoral companies. However, these gains were short-lived, as the pastoral companies continued after the war to refuse payment to their Aboriginal employees, despite the fact that beef became the Territory's major industry.

By the 1950s it became clear, the appalling state of Aboriginal health notwithstanding, that Aborigines were increasing in number at a faster rate than other Australians. They could no longer be ignored. The Government, working from the already outdated prewar proposals, passed the Welfare Ordinance in 1953—its objective assimilation, its guiding spirit paternalism. Introducing the new legislation the Minister for Territories, Paul Hasluck, said: 'In the course of time all persons of Aboriginal or mixed blood will live like white Australians do.'

Under this policy full-blood Aborigines remained wards of the State while half-castes were given full citizenship. The missions in Arnhem Land were retained as instruments of Government policy, forcing the remaining semi-nomadic Aborigines off their traditional land into conflict-ridden mixed-clan communities, mission clothes and meaningless work. Assimilation, in essence a form of racial discrimination, deprived the Aborigines of their traditional responsibilities and incentives and further stripped them of their identity and their land.

Arnhem Land until this time had been considered by most Europeans an inhospitable and inaccessible wasteland. In 1953, however, bauxite was discovered near Yirrkala in the east and further explorations led to the realization that the area contained some of the richest mineral deposits in the world. The more recent discovery of uranium in the west has potentially made Arnhem Land an economic trump card.

In order to mine the bauxite the Government resumed over 200 square kilometres of tribal land belonging to the people of eastern Arnhem Land and leased it to the giant Swiss company, Nabalco, thereby demonstrating that Aboriginal reserves were no longer inviolable. This threat to the reserves opened up the whole question of land rights and Aborigines throughout northern Australia began to organize deputations and protests in an attempt to gain formal recognition of these rights.

In 1963 the people of Yirrkala took a petition written on bark in the Gumatj language to Federal Parliament to protest against the resumption of their land. Their case went to the Supreme Court, but was lost on the grounds that under Australian law they had no title to the land. Later, despite legal challenges both in Australia and overseas, this decision was upheld and mining went ahead.

Three years later Gurindji stockmen and their families walked off the largest cattle station in Australia, Wave Hill, which is owned by the London-based Vestey Group. They set up camp on tribal land at Wattie Creek and petitioned the Governor-General to assist them in securing tenure. Nine years passed before the first legally recognized Aboriginal lease was handed over by the then Prime Minister Gough Whitlam to the Gurindji people in August 1975.

Meanwhile on Groote Eylandt Broken Hill Proprietary commenced manganese mining and built a township for 1,500 white employees. On Gove Peninsula Nabalco built a township for 5,000 whites only twenty kilometres from the Aboriginal settlement at Yirrkala. To the Aborigines the intrusion of these mining interests on their reserves

15 August 1975: Gough Whitlam picks up a handful of earth and hands it to Vincent Liangari, an elder of Gurindji tribe, to signify the first successful Aboriginal land rights claim in which a parcel of tribal land at Wave Hill Station was handed back to its traditional Aboriginal owners.

demonstrated the Government's lack of concern for them and its readiness to exploit the land at whatever cost.

In 1969 uranium was discovered in the west of Arnhem Land and it was estimated that the Alligator Rivers region alone contained some twenty per cent of the world's readily available deposits—for example the ore at Nabarlek is extremely high grade and possibly the richest in the world, although much larger tonnages exist on the edge of Arnhem Land at Jabiru and Jabiluka. According to Government estimates the uranium resources of this region could amount to ten times those identified so far.

In 1962 the Federal Government was pressured into amending the Aboriginal Ordinance to give all Aborigines the right to vote. Full Australian citizenship followed in 1964. Award wages were granted and the prohibition on the drinking of alcohol was lifted. A national referendum in 1967 gave the Commonwealth Government the right to overrule State Aboriginal legislation but in practical terms this meant little until the election of a Federal Labor Government in 1972.

The Labor Party wasted no time in implementing its policies for Aborigines. Prime Minister Gough Whitlam pledged to restore to Aboriginal people the lost power of self-determination in social, economic and political affairs. A department of Aboriginal Affairs was established in the Northern Territory where, unhampered by State legislation, Government policies were more effective than elsewhere. Once again the missions became the agents and administrators of Government policy in Arnhem Land: but the churches now had to support decentralization and the 'homelands movement' through which Aborigines could return to live in their traditional country; to permit the continuation and revival of cultural practices, and to make way for Aboriginal self-administration—all of which was a complete reversal of the previous assimilation policy.

A Commission was set up under Mr Justice Woodward to explore the matter of land rights and the Northern Land Council (NLC) was formed to state the Aboriginal point of view. At the same time a public enquiry directed by Mr Justice Fox sought to establish the environmental and social impact of uranium mining in the Alligator Rivers region of western Arnhem Land.

The Whitlam Government was short-lived and in 1975 the Liberal-National Country Party regained power. It was quick to announce its policy on Aboriginal affairs, stating that the Government would ensure that

traditional owners gained inalienable title to their land; the Aborigines would determine how their lands were to be used; would have the same right as any other landowner to determine who entered their land whether the person was Aboriginal or non-Aboriginal; and that sites significant according to Aboriginal tradition would be preserved and protected.

In theory this meant that Aborigines could veto minerals exploration and mining on their land; subsequent legislation, however, was to deny them this right.

As a result of the Woodward Commission's recommendations the *Aboriginal Land Rights (Northern Territory) Act* was passed in 1976. The Act, tempered somewhat by the change in government, recognized Aboriginal ownership of existing reserve land and laid down procedures whereby claims could be made to other traditional areas. Under the Act the NLC was formally recognized as a statutory body, able to bring land claims on behalf of Aboriginal people and by means of a statutory declaration to manage areas successfully claimed.

As the organization representing the traditional Aboriginal owners of the Alligator Rivers region, the NLC was obligated to negotiate with the mining companies on behalf of the traditional owners who had the right to veto mining on Aboriginal land. However, under certain exceptions, for example, mining leases held before the passage of the Act, the veto does not apply. This has complicated negotiations with multinationals such as Ranger Uranium and Pan Continental, which had discovered massive deposits of uranium oxide at Mt Brockman and Jabiluka.

During the Fox Inquiry, Silas Roberts, then the Maningrida representative for the National Aboriginal Conference, presented the Aboriginal point of view:

They say they will give us plenty of wages and jobs but we Aborigines do not think jobs and money are so important as our culture. Money cannot buy new culture . . . I say again, Aborigines do not like destroying land, especially near sacred sites [Mt Brockman is a sacred site.] It's like part of our body . . . how can we follow Aborginal tradition [if] we allow anything that hurts our land?

The Inquiry's report made it clear that mining in traditional tribal areas would damage the ecosystem on which the Aborigines depend, increase the risk to sacred sites, lead to racial tensions, lay the ground for alcohol abuse by aggravating sociological and psychological pressures, and undermine Aboriginal society through casual sexual associations between European men and Aboriginal women. Yet on 25 August 1977, Prime Minister Malcolm Fraser made the Government's attitude clear by announcing Australia's decision to enter the world market as a major uranium producer. Explaining his decision, he said: 'Australia has an obligation to provide the rest of the world with a vital source of energy. Only by supplying uranium can Australia have a voice in the world forums dealing with nuclear non-proliferation, effective safeguards and peaceful uses of atomic energy.'

Although the NLC had won its first claim for the traditional owners of vacant Crown Land around the East Alligator River, an area which included the 'uranium province', this new decision removed any hope that the Government would wholeheartedly uphold the recommendations of the Fox Report and thereby support the Aborigines in their negotiations with companies. Under the *Aboriginal Land Rights (NT) Act*, 1976, the NLC could only negotiate the terms, conditions and royalties involved in any agreement to mine but there is always the threat of Government intervention under the 'National Interest' clause: should the NLC and the mining companies fail to reach an agreement the Government retains the right to appoint an arbitrator.

Thus the mining companies and multinational corporations have moved into Arnhem Land. The land has been cut and opened.

Rum Jungle uranium mine 100 km south of Darwin is now closed but devastation caused by seepage from the tailings dam may last indefinitely.

1978

The escarpment towered above us, glaring in the midday sun. On the plains below swamp and bushland shimmered uninterrupted into infinity, a silent landscape seared into submission by the intensity of the sun. To our unaccustomed eyes and ears all life seemed obliterated by the heat. In reality, however, the silence was seething with life. Nearby two dark shapes raced up and down the red rock face: the shadows of sea eagles soaring in the sky above. Turning away from the escarpment, we forded the East Alligator River and crossed into Arnhem Land.

After eighteen months of planning and applying for permits, we had come—my colleague, Clive, our eighteen-month-old son Ben and I—to spend some time with the Aborigines, to work with bark painters, to explore and document the art and the way of life of the regions. We were not anthropologists, linguists, historians, teachers or missionaries: Clive was a video recordist and I am a photographer.

Past experiences with the media and other whites wielding cameras and recorders had left the Aborigines understandably fearful of being exploited, wary of anything that might disclose matters of a secret or sacred nature. In order to work in Arnhem Land we had agreed to submit our work to the community for approval before publication and to donate a selection of my slides and Clive's video tapes to the Australian Institute of Aboriginal Studies for possible future use by Aborigines themselves. However, despite these provisions it wasn't surprising that initially we were regarded with suspicion, not only by the Aborigines, but also by their white advisors.

For more than 40,000 years the Aborigines have been hunters and gatherers in this tropical region of coastal swamps, dense bushland and spectacular mountain ranges. The country is regarded with the greatest respect: survival in such a potentially hostile region has depended upon a deep understanding of the environment, a harmony with the elements and the forces of nature. However, the land is not only of economic importance; it also has great spiritual significance, for it is the very root of Aboriginal religion and the sacred law, the *Madayin*.

Over thousands of years the Aborigines had developed a strong oral tradition by which they maintained their religion, their history and their social order. Their history, which according to their belief system reaches to the very beginning of time, has been handed down through an elaborate complex of stories, song cycles and ritual. This belief system underpins Aboriginal society and preserves and reinforces the continuity of past and present.

In Arnhem Land today there are approximately 7,500 Aborigines comprising several hundred clans; over seventy different languages are spoken. Most Aborigines we met in central Arnhem Land spoke three or four different languages. Each person belongs to one major language group, but within this group there are many different clans, some of which have their own dialect. Almost all schooling is in English, which most of the younger generation now speak as a second language. The older people, however, use English only when they have to, and some not at all. Pidgin is not used in central Arnhem Land, but the 'work' English spoken by the people we met is highly idiomatic; in recording conversations I have used everyday English for clarity.

Our first rendezvous was with David Malangi, known to a handful of white Australians through his painting reproduced on the back of the one dollar note. An important and respected elder of the Liagalawumirri clan, Malangi lives in his own camp or 'homeland centre'—called an 'outstation' by whites—at Yatalemarra, 15 kilometres from the settlement at Ramangining.

After leaving the settlement we wove our way through the wet-season forest abundant with palms, flowers and tall grasses to Malangi's camp. Exotic water birds rose from the billabong as we approached and half a dozen camp dogs came barking out to greet us.

Malangi looked up from his bark painting and beckoned us to sit beside him on a blanket in the shade. Behind him sat two of his wives weaving pandanus dilly bags, while another, Gindjimirri, stirred the embers of a fire, put on a billy of tea, lit a long wooden pipe and passed it to her husband. After formal introductions Malangi drew on the pipe and passed it to us. Gazing out across the billabong where his young children splashed and romped as they searched for waterlily roots, he said, 'Before you start recording you must know about Yolngu people, about Arnhem Land.' (Yolngu is the word used by Aborigines in Arnhem Land to describe themselves.)

He told us about his country, his people and the Dreamtime long ago, when the mythological ancestors and supernatural creatures travelled across a flat and featureless land from sunrise to sunset. As they travelled, they searched for food, built shelters and had adventures. In each place where they stopped to dig for yams, hunt a kangaroo, spear a goose or throw away the bones of a fish, the landscape changed—a waterhole appeared, a rock formation grew or a sandbank rose from the sea. Each of these places became a sacred site and from these sites sprang the many clans of Arnhem Land.

'This is important story,' said Malangi watching us intently. 'This country here,' he tapped the ground with his pipe, 'is my mother's country; I am guardian for this country and for my people.'

Malangi went on to explain that the land is the very essence of the people who inhabit it. As a guardian of the land and of the *Madayin* he has an important role to pass on his knowledge to the younger generation, and to maintain the songs belonging to his clan country which are an integral part of an interrelated network of song cycles that follow the Dreaming tracks across Arnhem Land. Many songs sung today tell of the Creation and of the adventures of the Dreamtime ancestors. Others describe the land and its flora and fauna. There are songs too that tell of the *Baiini*, who visited Australia over a thousand years ago, arriving in their wide-beamed boats and bringing with them their women and children, their knowledge of cultivation and their weaving skills. Many songs recall the beauty and hardworking nature of the Baiini women. 'They must have been good women,' smiled Malangi, as he recalled a song that speaks of them as having 'buttocks like the sterns of their boats'.

Malangi returned to his painting, grinding the raw yellow ochre into powder on a slab of rock, mixing it with water and the traditional fixative—the juice of an orchid. Using a brush made from his daughter Muykul's hair, he painstakingly continued the delicate crosshatching. 'This painting,' he explained, 'is Milmildjark, my country, and

this,' pointing to the black circle in the centre, 'is my waterhole, a very sacred place.' As he described the features of his country he pointed to different parts of the semi-abstract painting. Slowly we began to 'read' the bark, learning to recognize the symbols of which it was composed.

Painting has always been an integral part of Aboriginal culture. Rock paintings were, and occasionally still are, a way of illustrating everyday happenings, of recording major events, of teaching the young about their culture and their past. Designs and sculptures in sand can perform similar functions. On ceremonial occasions painting is highly elaborate, being used to decorate sacred objects, the bodies of participants and the hollow logs used as coffins. The actual process of painting is a ritual within a ritual and as important as the finished work itself.

When the missions came they brought a cash economy with them, but offered little in the way of paid employment. Some of the early missionaries, seeing the potential of the medium, encouraged the Aborigines of Arnhem Land to produce bark paintings for sale and by 1978 art and craft sales provided one-sixth of the region's gross income.

Malangi, like every other painter, may paint only the stories and totems that belong to him, those which have been passed down to him from his parents. A typical painting may illustrate one or more of his totems or tell a story from his Dreaming. Malangi was at pains to impress upon us that the bark paintings he sells are 'public' or non-sacred, as opposed to the paintings used in ceremony and on sacred objects.

Some days later Malangi was called to a meeting of local traditional landowners whose country and waterways were being exploited by white commercial fishermen. He took a bark painting of his country with him to substantiate his ownership of certain tribal land. It had been arranged that while he was away we would go hunting with his younger brother, Gamarang, who was also a painter but his particular skill as a hunter required him to spend most of his time providing for the extended family at Yatalemarra.

He led us silently through the bush, into a swamp country that provides their most productive hunting ground. Stalking behind him among the cool paperbarks we responded to his signs and signals, learning from his every movement. A nod told us to wait, we slid behind a tree while the hunter, crouching, advanced on a flock of magpie geese feeding at a billabong. Their contented honking filled the stillness. We watched him approach from downwind, knee-deep in water, the tall reeds barely stirring above his head. He aimed and fired. A raucous cloud of birds took off, momentarily obliterating the sun, but Gamarang, his gun held above his head, was already wading towards the sounds of struggling and flapping among the reeds. Minutes later, soaked and smiling, he returned triumphant: six magpie geese with just one shot.

While hunting and painting are exclusively men's business, food gathering and weaving are women's business. The women at Yatalemarra are well known in the region for their weaving and during the next few days I was able to learn and record how it is done. With three of Malangi's wives, Gundbarra, Baypungala and Rogie, and several children, I set off through the bush to collect pandanus and bark fibre. The women carried machetes and down their backs hung long string dilly bags slung from their foreheads. Gundbarra warned me to be careful of snakes and to keep an eye out for orchids. 'We need that orchid root for making red colour,' she explained.

The palmlike pandanus grows abundantly in the swampy regions of Arnhem Land, but only the straight new fronds are suitable for weaving. The women cut the spiky metre-long leaves and stuffed them in their dilly bags, stopping from time to time to gather bush tucker and dig up orchid and other roots. When enough pandanus had been collected it was bound into bundles and carried back to camp on their heads. As only the centre of the leaf is good for weaving it has to be stripped while it is still fresh and supple. Gundbarra and Baypungala sat in the shade snapping the ends and rhythmically stripping away the spiny outer layers. 'Now you try,' Gundbarra said, passing me a bundle. It was only after I had wrecked a dozen leaves and had been much teased that I realized the skill this seemingly simple task required.

The usable fibre was dried in the sun until it closely resembled raffia. As colour plays an important part in the designs, some of it was then dyed. Baypungala scraped and pared the collected roots with the sharp edge of a sardine tin, tipping the peelings into two billies of water—orchid root for red, yam for yellow—in which the stripped fibre was placed to boil. Once dyed the fibre was hung to dry: once dry it can be kept and used at any time.

The traditional colours range from natural through yellow, orange and red to almost purple, according to the dyes available. Some weeks later at Kalobidada, I was shown a recent innovation: due to the lack of orchid root for red, Mary, who was making the dyes, brewed a billy of yellow; grinning mischievously she added a handful of washing powder and instantly the dye turned a brilliant red!

Pandanus fibre is woven by hand in a continuous circular form to produce useful items such as mats, baskets and dilly bags. Weaving styles and techniques vary according to region and the availability of materials. In drier regions 'bush string' is used instead of pandanus: bark fibre is stripped from melaleucas or tetradontas and pounded with the back of an axe into fibrous strands. It can then be coloured with root dye or by further pounding with crushed ochre, and the strands then spun into string by rolling up and down the thigh. (Sometimes goose down or orange parrot feathers are added to produce a feathered string much used in ceremony.) The string is 'crocheted' by hand into mesh bags. Bush string bags take longer to make but have the advantage of being enormously expansive, while pandanus dilly bags are closely woven and relatively rigid in shape.

Owing to the increasing demand by whites many of these woven items can now be sold to art and craft centres. The financial gain, though small in relation to the time and work involved, is not only an incentive to women to maintain their traditional skills; more importantly it returns to them some small degree of the economic independence their role as providers had once afforded them. In the missions and settlements this role has been undermined by the distance from any productive food-gathering grounds and the fact that the money needed to buy food from the store is earned mostly by men.

When next we saw Malangi, he was painting another bark, a lyrical piece depicting a tree, snakes, turtles and a stylized human being. This figure was Gurrumurringu, the first hunter of the Liagalawumirri clan. Malangi's father had told him this story, and he in turn had heard it from his father.

A long long time ago, Gurrumurringu went hunting and caught many geese and ducks. Later he became tired and hungry and stopped to rest beside a billabong, represented in the painting by crosshatching. 'This is a very sacred waterhole,' Malangi emphasized, explaining that it must never be contaminated. Beside it stood a sacred tree. Within the billabong lived the snake who had created the waterhole, while in the roots of the tree lived another. Malangi traced the outline of the snakes with his brush. Gurrumurringu made a big cooking fire beside the billabong, but the ashes from the fire fell on the water contaminating it, and the snakes rose up and killed him. Malangi took a one dollar note from his pocket and proudly explained that his painting on the back depicts the mortuary rites for Gurrumurringu.

Some weeks later, Malangi left for Milingimbi Island to take part in mortuary rites. We returned to Ramangining to look for George Milpurrur, a painter and an important local elder. He was reported to be in inaccessible country setting up an outstation, and was known only to see people when he felt like it. Fortunately we were able to arrange to visit his cousin, Johnny Bulun Bulun, at Mowemba, northwest of Ramangining.

The monsoonal rains had stopped and the bush tracks were slowly drying out as Clive, Ben and I set off along the ironically named 'Arnhem Land Highway' in search of Mowemba. During the wet season—December to March or April—the so-called highway, in reality no more than a track, is quite impassable; even in the dry season some stretches of it remain treacherous and boggy, and many of the rivers one has to cross are a hazard all year round. Eventually, seeing a signpost—the word 'Mowemba' chalked on a tree—we turned off the highway and followed some faint wheel-marks through the bush. For more than an hour of mistaken turnings and vanishing tracks we headed north, the dense bush gradually reducing to scrub before we finally arrived at a clearing. Two tents, some torn mosquito nets, the smouldering ashes of a fire and a radio aerial proclaimed that this was 'Somewhere'; but further investigation revealed only a fetid, leech-infested billabong and a million mosquitoes. If this *was* Mowemba, where was everybody?

We had seen one example of Bulun's work in Canberra—a four-metre-long bark, which we viewed under armed guard in the underground vaults of Australia's Department of Foreign Affairs. Now, six months and six thousand kilometres later, here we were in this abandoned swampland, Bulun Bulun's homeland, with our man apparently flown. There was nothing to do but wait.

The day dragged by to the drone of insects: there seemed

no escape from the relentless heat and whatever shade there was had already been claimed by the mosquitoes. At last a group of women and children returned. They made us welcome and soon after, as the sun went down, barking dogs and the chug of an engine announced another arrival. Minutes later, a tractor trundled out of the scrub. Jackie Wunawun and Johnny Bulun Bulun had returned, and with them our spirits. There was no doubt whose camp this was: Wunawun drove in like the hero in a Western, middle-aged, tall and handsome, wearing a white panama hat with a black band. Beside him rode Bulun Bulun, younger, shorter, stockier, his mop of long black hair tied with a green bandana, bandit-style. Wives, children and dogs rushed out to greet them.

That evening, sharing tea beside the fire, we learned that the men had been cutting tracks through the bush in preparation for an approaching ceremony. Wunawun was to be host for an important sacred ritual, the Kunapippi; it was now thirty years since the last such ceremony had been held at Mowemba by Jackie Wunawun's father. The responsibilities for the host are overwhelming. Not only must he organize the ceremony, but he must provide shelter, food and water for his several hundred guests; he must ensure that all the custodians of the songs are invited and arrive in time, play mediator between any jealous or rival clans, safeguard the secrets of the ceremony, instruct the young men in their roles and cut the time-hallowed tracks of the ancestors along which the initiates must travel to approach the ceremony ground. As the tracks had long since become overgrown, Wunawun was cutting a route through a hundred kilometres of virtually virgin bush, his only tools an axe, a rope and a tractor. Bulun Bulun was fully occupied helping Wunawun, but seemed amused and even flattered at the idea of assisting us to make an audio-visual about bark painting. He agreed to paint for us if in return we would help them with the use of our four-wheel drive vehicle.

Next morning Bulun Bulun arrived with an axe, saying, 'Now we go look for bark and I show you everything about bark painting.' He led us off through the bush, pointing out different trees and shrubs, explaining their numerous uses. He showed us softwood trees that are good for carving and the stringybark gums that are good for bark. He stopped to tap a branch, 'Listen here, this one is hollow, it is good for making didgeridoo. See how the tree is still

Most outstations in Arnhem Land own either a four-wheel drive vehicle or a boat. At Mowemba Outstation their workhorse is a tractor, driven here by Jackie Wunawun to collect firewood.

living, but white ants have eaten the inside.' He also explained that the tone of the 'doo alters depending upon its length.

Further on he found a straight and unblemished stringybark and with his axe made two incomplete rings in its bark, about two metres apart. He then made two vertical cuts between the rings and prised the bark away from the tree leaving a twenty-centimetre vertical strip of bark untouched. 'That piece,' he explained, 'must stay there to make the tree grow.' If the tree were ringed completely it would die. Bark can be peeled from the tree only when the sap is rising, so he cut a dozen barks that morning and we returned to Mowemba with a supply to last him through the dry season.

Back at the camp Bulun Bulun selected a large bark to paint, but first it had to be cleaned and straightened. He used a bush knife to scrape it smooth as canvas, then with the aid of fire—the Aborigines' most valuable tool—he straightened the bark and flattened it under a pile of logs. At this point his wife Nellie arrived, bearing a drum of water on her head and carrying a billy of tea. She was tall, with a striking resemblence to her brother Jackie Wunawun. She wore a long Indian skirt and puffed on a modern briar pipe which she passed to her husband as she invited us to share the tea. The children gathered round, squatting in the shade to watch the master at work.

In Arnhem Land only four colours are used in painting. Red and yellow are obtained from ochres found in rocky country throughout the region, white is provided by chalk or pipeclay found in river beds, and black comes from charcoal. The ochres are ground to a fine powder on a slab of rock and mixed with water and orchid-root fixative.

'First I cover all the bark with red ochre,' Bulun Bulun explained, fumbling in his dilly bag. 'You'd better not film this one,' he laughed, extracting an old shaving brush and dipping it into the paint. 'This one Balanda brush.' ('Balanda' comes from 'hollander', a word learnt by the Aborigines in their earliest contact with the Dutch and surviving as a designation for any foreigner or white man.) Bulun Bulun covered the bark surface and left it to dry. 'Now I show you proper Yolngu brush,' he said. Shredding some fine strands of bark fibre with a knife he bound them into a stick then dipped his new brush in the yellow ochre and with a bold and steady hand drew a circle in the centre of the bark. 'This is a waterhole,' he said, explaining that

water is the source of all life. Meticulously he outlined the symbols for springs and watercourses and drew his totems: turtles, geese, snakes and flying foxes. Soon the entire bark was covered with strong, fluid lines that formed an intricate and subtle design.

Over the next few days we sat with Bulun Bulun while he worked, recording his brushwork on film and his explanations on tape as he elaborated on the design and embellished the symbols with crosshatching. He summoned his nine-year-old son Johnny to sit with him. 'My son goes to school,' he said proudly. 'He's learning to read and write whitefella way, but he must learn Yolngu way too, learn about his Dreaming and his country.'

At dusk each evening Bulun Bulun and Wunawun would join us round the camp fire for a while, then politely take their leave and disappear into the bush for 'men's business'. One night we were honoured with an invitation to join in. Wunawun led Clive to the men at the ceremony ground while Nellie, his sister, led me to the women's camp.

It was a dark, moonless night. In the smoky glow of a ring of smouldering logs, a group of women and children sat huddled in a semi-circle. Nellie and I joined them, nursing our sleeping children in our laps. The girls cuddled up close to whisper and giggle. An elderly woman sang and beat a rhythm on the ground, the others joining in and encouraging the girls to dance. Shy and giggling they followed the older women, copying their every movement, shuffling and stamping in the mingled smoke and dust. Occasionally one of the women would writhe erotically, provoking shrieks of joy and wild applause. The pounding of their feet soon formed a mound between two parallel trenches, a mound which, the women explained, was considered sacred for the duration of the ceremony.

Suddenly a distant cry cut through the performance. The women hushed. From somewhere beyond the darkness an eerie call penetrated the night—a message from the men's camp. The women responded with a spinechilling shrill, creating a momentary link between these separate yet interdependent rituals. The dance resumed; there was a sense of timelessness, a blending of past, present and future. After several hours it stopped abruptly. We bundled up our children and dispersed in the darkness to our tents. Each night for several months these rites would be performed. As the younger ones gradually learnt from their elders, the ritual

20

would be reinforced and the ancient knowledge passed on.

We were only allowed to leave Mowemba after promising to be back, as Wunawun put it, 'In time for the full moon, not the next one, but the one after.' It was then that the ceremony would reach its climax. We set out reluctantly, accompanied by the barking dogs and shouts of '*Bo bo*' (farewell), and headed east for the settlement at Maningrida.

Maningrida is a sprawling government settlement 500 kilometres east of Darwin on the north coast of Arnhem Land. It was set up in 1959 as part of the then Liberal-National Country Party Government's assimilation plan, and unlike the church settlements is administered by bureaucrats and specialists from the Department of Aboriginal Affairs.

With a population of 400 Aborigines and 100 whites, a school for 200 children and jobs available for Aborigines, Maningrida is a township with a distinctive tempo and rhythm, neither Aboriginal nor white. Although it is cut off by road for three months of the year, there are daily flights to Darwin, a supply barge once a month and a radio telephone link to the world beyond.

The settlement's short history is littered with discarded assimilation schemes, development theories and money-making enterprises. The township, in which a dozen different clans jostle for identity, bears witness to these abandoned experiments: the expensive sawmill, long since closed, provides the children with an adventure playground; the welfare kitchen has become a store; the pottery workshop and market gardens have been reclaimed by the bush, the old timber houses replaced by Darwin-style ones; all that remains of the fishing fleet is a rusting hulk stranded in the mud of the estuary. Maningrida has cost millions and still remains impoverished.

European influences have undoubtedly brought some benefits: education, medical care and religion have introduced support systems that have now been absorbed into traditional Aboriginal structures; housing, transport, electricity and the general store play a major role in the lives of many Aborigines, but in a society traditionally geared to a complex system of sharing, these assets have also imposed new and unfamiliar responsibilities. The result, in many cases, has been conflict and confusion, both at the family level and in the Aboriginal community as a whole.

In the early years the frustration of static settlement liv-

ing, the loss of immediate hunting grounds, dependency on a cash economy and the confusion which stems from inter-clan rivalries, caused tension and a breakdown of traditional social order and of the law which once maintained it. For some alcohol provided a temporary escape from this bewildering existence, but binges in the towns led to conflict with whites and Australian law. Alcohol began to be secreted back into the communities and in some settlements was permitted (within limits) as the lesser of two evils. However, a rise in crime and violence resulted, the situation being exacerbated when many of the children took to petrol sniffing. By the late 1960s many families were looking for an alternate way of living.

Here the money that had brought with it so many problems actually proved useful. Vehicles could be bought and families thus enabled to renew their relationship with distant clan country. For many Aborigines these visits became longer: seasonal camps were set up for hunting and for ceremony business, and what became known as the 'homelands movement' began. With the change of Federal Government in 1972 funds were made available for the establishment of outstations; there are now a hundred of them in Arnhem Land, home to two-thirds of the region's Aboriginal population.

However, despite many changes, major problems still exist. In Arnhem Land, as in Aboriginal communities throughout Australia, health is still a serious concern as is demonstrated by the fact that the life expectancy of Aborigines is some twenty years less than that of other Australians; the infant mortality rate is about three times that of whites; trachoma is 15% more prevalent in Aborigines than non-Aborigines (in the Northern Territory about 70% of all Aborigines are affected); the leprosy rate is still one of the highest in the world and many Aboriginal children suffer from otitis media (ear disease) which results in some degree of hearing loss.

Since the establishment of the Department of Aboriginal Affairs in 1968 large amounts of money have been poured into medical services in Arnhem Land providing substantially increased facilities, services and special care. Even though each settlement and mission has a clinic (and a few have a hospital) there are no resident doctors and patients with serious conditions have to be flown to Darwin or Gove for treatment, a solution which is both alien and frightening for many Aborigines. Also, despite the increased services and facilities many people feel that they are neither satisfactory nor relevant to their needs. Many Aborigines are afraid of Western medicine and feel intimidated by the clinics and the impersonal treatment especially as hospitalization represents isolation from their families and the possible threat of intrusion into their personal life (for example, family planning). Thus many people are deterred from reporting their illness until it becomes acute and many will only call upon the nurse at the clinic after they have first sought help from their own medicine men and women. However, as many of the diseases suffered by Aborigines have been introduced since settlement there are no effective traditional treatments for them.

Until recently the lack of respect and understanding shown by white medical personnel for traditional Aboriginal medical practices further alienated their patients. However, since the early 1970s an attempt has been made to train Aboriginal health workers, while more interest in traditional Aboriginal medicine is now sometimes shown by white health professionals. The trainee health workers not only provide a vital link between the white staff and their patients by being able to interpret in the patients' language, they can explain some of the psychological and cultural factors involved in certain cases. Once trained in basic health care many of the trainees return to their homelands where they can provide an important field service by treating minor ailments themselves and referring more serious cases to the nearest clinic.

Another continuing problem is malnutrition, not because people are actually starving but because the introduction of a sedentary lifestyle and the availability of certain foods have drastically affected Aboriginal diet. Some obvious examples of this are the problems caused by the over use of white sugar and white flour. In the past flour for making damper (unlevened bread) was obtained either from grass seeds or cycad nuts. The process was long and laborious, the former producing a flour full of roughage and the latter taking five days to prepare. I had one experience of making a damper the 'old way'. First we gathered several dilly bags and billy cans of green cycad nuts, then with the aid of two stones, one serving as palette and the other as hammer we cracked open the nuts, removed the kernels and peeled off their brown protective skins. The white kernels were then placed in a bush-string dilly bag which was left in a nearby spring for five days to remove all traces of poison. At the end of this time the sodden, smelly pulp was pummelled into a dough and baked in the ashes of a fire to produce a bitter-tasting, tough 'bread'. Five days to wait for a slice of bread and no jam!

Now it is different: white flour is used to make the damper which has become the basis of Aboriginal diet. In some settlements white sliced loaves are available to be eaten with large quantities of golden syrup or dipped in white sugar. In the past sugar-bag, the wild bush honey, was the only sweet bush food. It provided energy and was considered a delicacy. It was hard to find and even harder to extract, usually demanding several hours' labour, and therefore it was only rarely consumed. No wonder then, that when white sugar and sweetened foods were introduced the Aborigines found them irresistible.

Despite the fact that most Aborigines have a weakness for things sweet, paradoxically they don't have appalling teeth. The visiting dentist at Ramangining believes this is because most Aboriginies still *use* their teeth. Bush tucker, raw meat, nuts, roots and bones when still important in the diet all help to keep the teeth healthy and strong, despite the lack of toothbrushes.

In Maningrida we collected mail, rented rooms, took numerous showers, slept between sheets, consumed vast quantities of Coca-Cola and nauseating meat pies, bought supplies, recharged our equipment and by some ridiculous force of our conditioning, availed ourselves of every modern facility. Aware of the gap between the culture we were a part of and the one we had come to Arnhem Land to explore, we took off again after three days and headed for Kalobidada.

Kalobidada is an outstation 130 kilometres south-west of Maningrida and the home of Wally Mandarg, a respected leader of the Rembarnga clan. Mandarg is now over seventy, a renowned tribal doctor and well-known painter who shuns contact with whites and speaks no English. Once a pastrycook in a mission settlement, he was the first to return to his clan country, setting up his own camp near the Cadell River twenty years ago. He lives with his four wives, some of his twenty children and other relatives and encourages his family to be self-sufficient and to adhere closely to traditional values.

At Kalobidada, near the abundance of the river a dozen bark huts sheltered in a sandy clearing. An emu strolled around the camp and a mob of dogs came bounding out to meet us. Mandarg was painting in the shade of his bark hut while close by a group of his sons played didgeridoo and sticks. After formal introductions and the sharing of sweet billy tea, we were allotted a spot to camp. The hospitality was overwhelming. The men assisted us in erecting a bough shade, the women offered us rakes to clear the ground, and the children, curious to play with Ben, brought firewood. Later Becky, Mandarg's daughter, helped me bake a damper.

Mandarg summoned the men to a conference to discuss plans for our stay and Becky's husband, Jimmy Singleton, acted as interpreter: 'Old man says, first you must understand about our land, the land is very important to Aboriginal people. Then we will show you something about our culture.' It was decided that we should first of all visit Rembarnga rock country, the country of Mandarg's ancestors and of the Mimi spirits.

Next morning we were up with the sun and accompanied by three of Mandarg's sons, their wives and children, we set off through tangled rainforest and majestic paperbark swamps. An hour later we emerged into the blinding sunlight: all around us were towering red rocks, crystal pools and cool, dark caverns. On the side of a rock a notice proclaimed: THIS OUR SACRED REMBARNGA COUNTRY KEEP OUT. We stopped at this favourite Rembarnga camping spot for tea and a swim. The women decided to stay here for the day, fishing for yabbies (freshwater crayfish) and gathering 'bush tucker', while the men took us further into their country.

Up rock faces, through narrow gorges, past caves and burial grounds, Jimmy, Jackie and Paddy led us to a site high in the escarpment, a vast overhanging gallery alive with layers of paintings. A life-sized kangaroo, a giant barramundi and erotic human figures represented the work of Mandarg over many years. Through them wove the faded paintings of the ancestors and the faint, fluid lines of the Mimi figures—capricious spirits—painted long ago in blood. Proudly, Jackie told us about the paintings, about the ancestors and their exploits.

Throughout Australia, paintings in caves and rock galleries tell of incidents and events that happened long ago. Rock paintings found in north-east Arnhem Land show the arrival of the Macassans in their multi-sailed 'praus'. They depict these visitors at work, the prayer man (the Macassans were Muslims) calling from the mast of a boat, and one even provides an accurate cross-section of a prau with all its contents. The Macassans made seasonal visits over many centuries and their way of life and their relationship with the coastal people of Arnhem Land are still remembered in the songs and dances of the region.

Further west, in the escarpment country, numerous rock paintings illustrate the arrival of the white men. Whites were often painted with their hats on, as though these were extensions of the body. They are often shown with horses and guns and many of the paintings clearly depict the conflict that accompanied the intrusion of these 'Balanda' invaders.

Here, however, there were no obvious signs of strangers. All around us on the gallery floor lay a bed of loose flint pieces. 'This is a very special stone,' said Jackie, leading us to an outcrop of hard white rock. 'This rock is very sharp, we use it for making spears and for making young men.' He took a sliver of stone and ran it lightly across his arm; a fine line of blood oozed from the hairline cut. 'This stone is sharper than those Balanda blades, makes better cut, proper Yolngu way.' The three men proudly displayed the deep scars across their chests which distinguish them as 'full men'—men who have gone through the many stages of initiation and tribal law. Jimmy explained that this sharp stone was very rare, and that this place had been a source of spear heads, axes and cutting tools for thousands of years. Rembarnga people have traditionally traded these tools not only with their neighbours in Arnhem Land, but also with the desert people further south in exchange for boomerangs and other desert goods. Interestingly, however, boomerangs are never used for hunting in Arnhem Land, perhaps because the country is too densely treed. They are prized for use in ceremony as clap-sticks and should remain hidden from women and uninitiated boys.

Throughout the day the men pointed out sites of importance, and told us stories of their ancestors. We encountered rock wallabies, pigeons, lizards, a goanna and a cave full of flying foxes. They stopped to show us fruit, flowers and insects, encouraging us to try the edible ones while pointing out others prized for their medicinal or magical powers. We tasted wild honey, swam after fish in rocky pools, listened to echoes, ate witchetty grubs and finally scrambled to the top of a solitary outcrop of rock. In a crevice beneath a painted overhang lay a hollow log coffin blackened with age. 'This one our granny,' said Jimmy. 'He *is* Mandarg's father, he was a very important man, we put him here because this is his country, his Dreaming place.' As Jackie and Jimmy explained about mortuary rites, the painting of the coffin and the songs that 'sing' a deceased person back to the land of his ancestors, Paddy picked up a couple of sticks and softly began to accompany them with song. Soon all the men were singing and we were back with the Mimi spirits in the timeless past.

We returned to Kalobidada as the sun was setting and found the camp busy with pre-dusk fervour, the women raking the ground clean, collecting firewood and baking damper. The children were busy in the bush setting light to leaves and clumps of grass, ostensibly to ward off the mosquitoes but managing meanwhile to create their own display of fireworks.

Mandarg decided there should be a *bunghl* that evening for our benefit and soon after dinner the click of sticks ricocheted through the darkness, inviting us to his camp to join the singing and dancing. In the firelight Mandarg presided silently while his sons took turns singing and playing the didgeridoo; in the shadowy background the women danced their sedate, shuffling steps in time with the songs. 'This song is about the barramundi,' Jimmy explained. 'That's Mandarg's Dreaming.' The dancers whirled and stamped in the dust as the onlookers called out encouragement and applause. Then, as the fires died down the children were dispatched to bed and the adults drew closer to share tea and the latest information on local issues. The immediate concern was a new trend in the administration of the outstation movement. Jimmy was keen to point out to us how the movement was vital to their survival, a means to maintain Aboriginal law and social order: 'This way we can live proper Aboriginal way, keep our ceremonies and be strong.' Then he added, 'You can tell those Balanda down south, Arnhem Land is Aboriginal land, belongs to Aboriginal people.'

Although most outstations own either a boat, tractor or four-wheel drive vehicle the demand on them is excessive, the terrain punishing and many are frequently out of action. (Locals estimate the lifespan of a truck in this area is only nine months.) To overcome some of these logistical hazards many outstations are cutting their own emergency airstrips. However, the most important feature of every outstation is its two-way radio. Powered by a 12-volt battery it provides a vital communication link with others in the bush and with the settlements.

From dawn to dusk the radio clamours with chatter, gossip and vital information, in English and a variety of local languages, interspersed with wartime radio jargon.

One morning as we clustered round the crackling radio Jimmy was called by Maningrida. The gentle bushman suddenly became business-like as he strained to catch the message and shouted his response. He turned to us wearily and said, 'Got to go to Maningrida, some trouble there I've got to sort out.' As the current chairman of the Outstation Resource Association, he explained, 'Our job is to help the outstations. We help them to be self-sufficient, and to make decisions, but all the time there are too many worries, too many problems.'

During our stay at Kalobidada, Ben and I spent many days with the women and children learning bush crafts and gathering bush tucker. They introduced me to the berries, nuts and roots that provide the basic Aboriginal diet; showed me how to catch turtles and freshwater prawns; to gather yams, snails and lily corms, and took me on expeditions in search of wild honey known as sugar-bag.

At Kalobidada, as at many other outstations, traditional education is encouraged, the children learning bushcraft, cultural practices and responsibilities from their elders; discovering nature, playing music and learning songs.

European schooling is haphazard and informal, conducted in the shade of a large ironwood tree by one of the young mothers, Rita, who has the unenviable task of rounding up the children and maintaining their attention amidst the bush distractions. A tin trunk, full of books and crayons is the school's only piece of furniture and once a fortnight in the dry season a white teacher from Maningrida arrives to replenish the supplies and reinforce the system. The teacher is greeted with great enthusiasm but the relevance of the three Rs is shortlived when there are lizards to spot or goannas to chase and the entire country is their playground.

Some families we met who lived on outstations wanted formal European education for their children. However, this often required the children, and sometimes their mothers, to camp with relatives in the settlements during the week, which put extra pressure not only on their own family relationships but also on those of their relatives.

The outstation resource centre in Maningrida services approximately 25 outstations and once a fortnight despatches—tracks permitting—supplies and mail by truck to each outstation. One afternoon during our stay at Kalobidada the children heard a vehicle approaching and anticipating supplies the whole camp poured out to meet it. Jimmy Singleton took charge of the business side, witnessing the thumb prints and identification marks of Mandarg and the old women as they claimed their pension cheques and the signatures of younger women collecting their child endowment. On outstations no one receives dole cheques, but like all Australians Aboriginal people are entitled to widow's, old age and single-parent pensions. The cash was then shared throughout the camp. The women bought food—flour, tea, sugar, tins of spaghetti and camp pie and maybe a new dress or blanket, while the children dived amongst the throng for lollies, fishing lines and anything that took their fancy. The men bought cartridges, tobacco and bush knives, indulged in a new stetson, and some bought a case of non-alcoholic cider.

On outstations the incentive and opportunity to drink are greatly reduced, not only by the remoteness of the location but, more importantly, by the sharing of responsibilities and by a new-found pride in the traditional values. Nonetheless, as a result of continuous alcohol-related problems the Aboriginal Councils in Arnhem Land have banned liquor from outstations, and most of the missions and settlements are theoretically 'dry'.

At Kalobidada, the men went hunting every few days. Shotguns and vehicles make their task easier, but when they ran out of cartridges they used a variety of spears depending on whether their game was kangaroo, goose or emu. Fishing lines and lures are used in deep water for catching barramundi, but in shallow water the two-pronged spear is still the most efficient fishing tool.

When hunting was not the top priority, the men would paint, make spears and prepare for ceremonies, but much of their time was spent in discussion—debate on the politics of Aboriginal life, kinship, marriage diplomacy, land rights, law old and new, and the changing nature of their society. One obvious area for consideration is that of the conflict between the generations. The younger people with their European education and better understanding of white culture, have the potential to undermine the authority of their elders, but anthropologists say there is little evidence that this is happening. On the contrary, there appears to be a concerted effort to find a compromise encompassing both the old and the new.

Many of the younger men with whom we had lengthy discussions were determined to find a solution to the problem. Twenty-four-year-old Tony Binalany, for example, works as Community Development Officer at Ramangining and has attended conferences and seminars in Australia and overseas. As he explained, 'It is a hard job for me. I am only a young man, not full-man yet, but I have to stand between all that white business and the old men. It is a big responsibility and some people don't like that.' However, he explained that adherence to the *Madayin*, the sacred law, did not preclude change in customary law. The introduction of the European legal system has often led to confusing changes in customary law, but he emphasized that it need not undermine the *Madayin*, the kinship system or the basic principles of Aboriginal society.

Binalany plays an interesting role in changing Aboriginal society. Not only is he destined to be a custodian of traditional law, he is also a practising Christian.

In the late 1970s the Aboriginal Evangelical Fellowship took root on Elcho Island and has since sung its way into and through all the communities in Arnhem Land. At 10 o'clock one night in Ramagining a crescendo of amplified Hallelujahs and Praise the Lord's rent the silence. Investigation of this wild but joyful intrusion revealed half the population gathered under the tin roof of the community shelter in vigorous worship. Lights blazed as half a dozen young men plucked their electric guitars while men in one group and women and children in another clapped and sang in harmony, calling out to the Lord and acting out the numerous revival songs. Most songs were sung in English but some had been translated into Guparpyngu by the local missionaries. A few had been composed by the Aborigines themselves and described their own community. The simple hymns were delivered in lusty five or six part harmonies and were interspersed with prayers, sermons, bible reading, incantations and swooning. Each phase of the ritual was applauded with 'Praise the Lord' and choruses of 'Amen'. When one young woman collapsed in a faint of religious rapture the spirit of our Lord was seen to have entered her being and the fellowship was considered to have been successful.

David Malangi with wives Elsie (left) and
Baypungala (right) and two of his daughters,
Muykul and May, at their outstation at
Yatalemarra.

Not a night passed at Ramangining without some form of Fellowship taking place, even during ceremony time, and during the day the young men fervently practised their music while many of the young women recited hymns and prayers at home from tapes. Once a week enthusiastic members of the Fellowship would go to one of the homeland centres to spread the word of God. While enjoying the unusual entertainment some of the old men viewed the new rage with scepticism. As one wise elder said, 'It keeps the kids out of mischief, it doesn't seem to do any harm, but its all Balanda business, not Aboriginal way.'

On outstations in central Arnhem Land information from outside is limited to schoolbooks, mission literature, Christian comics and occasional Kung-fu movies shown in the settlements. There is no Aboriginal radio service, newspapers rarely get beyond the settlements and the regular radio transmissions from Darwin can be picked up only on the most sophisticated radio receivers. Their strong oral tradition and the speedy dissemination and transmission of information between outstations by two-way radio keep people in regular contact with each other and occasionally the world beyond.

In 1978 while the debate about uranium mining raged across Australia, in Arnhem Land the lack of information about mining and land rights was alarming. What little news filtered through to outstations was often considered 'Balanda business'. Pressure from outside was growing rapidly, but many outstation people were unaware of the effect development and political change could have on their lives. The Uniting Church distributed pamphlets about uranium, but most of the people we met on outstations around Ramangining and Maningrida had no conception of the environmental and social effects of mining. When in September numerous telegrams arrived from white organizations in the south supporting the Aborigines' stand against uranium, they were totally baffled. Unaware that they had any friends in the white community outside Arnhem Land, it was inconceivable to them that people they did not know, were not kin, nor of the country could be concerned about them and their problems. It was, however, equally inconceivable that white men could be so foolish as to want to dig up a sacred site as important as Mt Brockman.

As we sat round the camp fire one night only seventy kilometres east of Mt Brockman, a young man asked, 'Everyone talking about that uranium for making bombs. What do they want those bombs for?' A long discussion followed in which some of the older men, who remembered the Japanese bombings, explained about Balanda warfare. Njimininuma, a friend of ours, laughed and said, 'Well, we're not like Indians any more, we've got guns, we're like cowboys now, like Balanda.'

'But whitefella once used spears and axes too,' I pointed out.

Njimininuma was incredulous, 'But whiteman, he *always* had gun.'

Trying to explain, I described an ancient castle near my home in England where during medieval times white men used cannon balls and burning tar, whereupon the men collapsed in disbelieving laughter. Njimininuma was about forty, his Dreaming is crocodile, and as an expert on crocodiles he had worked closely with Government researchers; but his lack of English and of formal schooling meant that his knowledge about things outside his world was limited.

Like many other Aborigines we met he was not to remain so innocent for long. Unknown to any of us that night his land was already under threat, having been earmarked for mining exploration.

Discussion, Aboriginal style, is a lengthy and time-consuming process; however, since time is unimportant, decisions can wait until every person has had his or her say. The process is full of oblique personal opinions. As the discussion widens, and even when the conclusion is already obvious, opinions may need to be sought from persons not immediately at hand. Consensus, therefore, takes time. It is a truly democratic process, often masterfully managed; indeed the process is frequently more important than the outcome, which, after days of talking, may still be inconclusive.

In Aboriginal society important knowledge is transmitted, re-enacted and revivified through ritual and ceremony. As knowledge is acquired through life experience and through 'business' its transmission is dependent upon the wise and knowledgeable—often, but not necessarily, the older generation.

Sacred knowledge belongs to all Aboriginal people, but is not directly available to all: it is not a 'possession' to be coveted, a means of self-aggrandizement, it is gained in order to pass on, the custodians holding it in trust for the younger generation. Should sacred knowledge be misused by an individual, punishment will follow. The punishment for most transgressions against Aboriginal law is decided by a consensus of opinion, although sometimes punishment may be postponed until it can be considered by others. During times of ceremony, when large numbers of initiated people are gathered, major events, issues and transgressions are openly discussed. Ceremony thereby provides a forum for resolution or absolution of transgressions and this communal judgement itself acts as a deterrent against many forms of incorrect behaviour. It is however, ineffective against the newer problems of drunkenness and delinquency.

My initial impression of Aboriginal society in Arnhem Land was that it was not only patriarchal but also chauvinistic and that decision making appeared to be 'men's business'. Slowly, however, as I began to understand the subtleties and structure of their social order I came to realize that some of this apparent male chauvinism is a reflection of the Christian ethic and other European influences.

In traditional Aboriginal society, men and women had clearly defined roles and responsibilities which conferred on each a separate independence. Women maintained an economic independence as providers and food gatherers, and in addition had a social responsibility as the nurturers of community well-being. Not only did they 'grow-up' their children, they also 'grew up' their knowledge of the land and passed it on. Women's ritual and ceremonial business centred on the health of country and community, while men fulfilled the role of hunters, warriors, politicians and guardians of the *Madayin*. Survival was the objective and in this women played an equal part. Their views could not be ignored. The balance of power was maintained by co-operation and the division of responsibility.

The coming of Europeans upset this balance. Christianity, European law, colonialism and attempts at assimilation all embodied, utilized and reinforced the notion of male supremacy. Male administrators, male anthropologists and male preachers all sat down and talked with male Aborigines. The nature of the Aboriginal social order, with its avoidance relationships and taboos that dictate which men and which women may sit down together, inevitably meant that women were excluded from most of these dis-

cussions. Decisions were made by men amongst men, and as mentioned earlier, the traditional female role as a provider was undermined by the cash economy. Thus, since contact with whites began, the role of men has been emphasized and that of women played down.

Aboriginal society does, however, have some inherently patriarchal aspects, one of which is the traditional custom of arranged marriages. Aboriginal law provides an intricate and sophisticated structure for correct partnerships, adherence to which has prevented incest and inbreeding over tens of thousands of years. Effective as a system for survival, arranged marriages can also be used for increasing the power of an individual or clan, with young girls becoming mere pawns. Aboriginal law in Arnhem Land defines precisely who is permitted to marry whom according to kinship status. Since an individual's skin status is determined by that of his parents, marriages can be arranged even before a child's birth. It was customary for girls to be married to their second cousins, which frequently meant that the older men would claim their promised wives soon after the girls reached puberty. Secret love-relationships and extramarital affairs did (and do) occur, but the deterrent was strong for punishment was banishment or spearing.

Today, things are changing as Australian law, co-education, and the example of white behaviour all undermine the old law. Many young men and women now want partners of their own choice, and some of the older women are objecting, heedless of clan diplomacy, to their teenage daughters becoming the youngest wives of elderly men.

Mandarg's daughter, Lyn, seventeen, has her own doubts about the promised marriage system. 'I want to go to school and learn to be a health worker, maybe get married later,' she told us. Mary, another sister, is twenty-nine and adamant that she will not marry: 'I want to stay here with my family. My mother Rosie is getting old. I must look after her. Anyway, I don't want to be slave to any man.' She already has two children by a 'wrong-skin' relationship, and after several years of banishment has now been accepted back into the family.

Marriage is a dilemma, too, for the young man who, in his mid-twenties, would like to take a wife and yet may be bound by a promise—made by someone else on his behalf—to a little girl of only four or five. So the debate about marriage goes on as the elders try to find a compromise. The rules are beginning to relax and young people may soon be allowed more freedom in their choice of partners, as long as they adhere to the correct relationships.

Kinship and what is known as the 'skin system' not only provide a set of rules as to how people should relate to each other, they also impose responsibilities and obligations. Within this framework individuals both provide and are provided for in a survival-oriented extended family. During our first few months in Arnhem Land, the elders at Ramangining decided to include us in this system by giving us skin names that would enable clan members to relate to us in a socially appropriate way. We knew nothing about how this decision came about. Bulain, Dhartangu, Malangi and others decided that Clive was of the Dhuwa moiety, skin name 'Burralang', and that I, as his defacto wife had to be of the opposite Yirritja moiety and one of the two permitted skin choices, 'Bulandjan' or 'Ngaritjan'. When it was decided that I was to be 'Bulandjan', Ben automatically became 'Wamut'. Acceptance of this new status meant that according to Aboriginal law we had certain obligations and responsibilities to our new relations, as they did to us. It meant in practice that wherever we went and whomever we met we had classificatory relations. On introducing myself as Bulandjan to a group of complete strangers, I would be greeted with, 'Hey, Bulandjan, you must be my mother!' or 'You're my sister, aunty, granny, daughter!'

I was no sooner rejoicing in my new-found status than its restrictions suddenly hit me. Both Bulain and Milpurrur, with whom we were working are Bulain—my classificatory brothers. Aboriginal law demands an avoidance relationship between brothers and sisters (as between sons and mothers-in-law), which meant that theoretically I could not speak their names, nor look them in the face. For a moment I saw the whole project falling apart. How was I to work with Milpurrur and Bulain?

We sat down with Bulain to discuss the problem. I held my breath as he spelled out the letter of the law and then with much merriment made light of our dilemma by saying it was okay for me to photograph him because I was only looking at him through my camera! I breathed again, but a moment later was rebuked for offering him a cigarette. Laughing, he demanded that I throw the cigarettes to him instead of passing them, thereby observing at least part of the taboo. I got the message and played the game. With Bulain it became a continuous joke, a provocative

game, but I was careful not to overstep the mark and to remember my role as sister. Ultimately, however, it was Ben, 'Little Wamut', who really established a place for us: playful and adventurous, he cemented relationships without inhibition.

By the time we returned to Ramangining in July 1978, we had something to show for all the snapping and shooting of our first visit—videotapes, recordings and photographs. Whatever suspicion and mistrust there has been in the beginning evaporated in the excitement that accompanied the first tentative showing of our work to Malangi and his family. This demonstration and their comprehension of the idea of an audio-visual display to accompany exhibitions of bark painting suddenly gained us their support. Invitations to visit other outstations followed and some days later, after a two-hour boat trip down the Glyde River and along the north coast of Arnhem Land, we arrived at Dippirringur, an outstation on the coast and home of the painter Binyinuwuy.

Here above the dazzling white beaches and the irridescent azure sea a tiny encampment of tin sheds sheltered in the sand dunes under tamarind and casurina. The desert island image whooped into life as a dozen naked children streaked down the beach to the boat. Curious and surprised they watched us unload our cases and cartons of equipment. No dogs heralded our arrival. Balang later explained: 'I don't allow dogs here, they make too much trouble. Impossible to keep a clean camp with dogs. They dig up all the garbage, fight for it and dump it all over the place.' Once dogs would have assisted cleaning up a camp because every leftover was edible, but the introduction of packaged food, cans and plastic containers has created a new 'modern' problem for the other outstations.

That night we camped alongside Balang and his family on the dunes above the sea. At dawn, just as I was steeling myself to brave the mosquitoes in a search for firewood, I heard the snap and crackle of sticks outside our tent. A voice called, 'Breakfast time, Bulandjan, breakfast time,' and there was Binyinuwuy's wife Morpindi, bearing a billy of steaming tea and stoking our fire. Moments later she came again with fresh damper and a tin of treacle in a generous ritual which continued throughout our stay.

During the following days we spent much of our time

with Balang, sitting in the shade of a tamarind, recording his work on a large bark painting that reaffirmed the story of the morning star. 'You know that time before the sun comes up,' he asked, gazing out across the sea, 'when the moon is fish again and swimming in the ocean? That is the time, our ancestors tell us, when Barnambirr, the morning star, is released from her woven dilly bag on that faraway island of Baralku. Behind that morning star trails a feathered string.' He pointed to a white design on the partly completed bark. 'That string is tying her to her home, holding Barnambirr low in the sky. That string of light from Barnambirr that falls on the sea is called Jari, and the spirits of the dead follow Jari back to Baralku, the island beyond the sunrise, to join their ancestors of the Dreamtime.'

Everywhere we went in Arnhem Land these fine threads of Aboriginal mythology, the invisible web of the Dreamtime, wove in and out of daily life. For everything there is an explanation, a story, a song or a dance, and sometimes a ritual, giving meaning and significance to everything that exists.

Some weeks later we returned to Mowemba for the final rites of the Kunapippi. The family camp had expanded to accommodate several hundred guests in an all-embracing mêlée of excitement. Clive had joined the men, and Gundbarra, Malangi's wife and my skin aunt, assumed the role of mother, helping me to set up camp beside the Yatalemarra women, while Muykul and May took Ben off to play. After sunset, in the lingering magenta glow, red ochre was slapped on bodies and smeared on hair in an all-female ritual within a ritual, a laughing, joking sharing of the last night of the 'business'.

The Kunapippi ceremony itself I am not permitted to describe, but that night something extraordinary took place. Ben and I sat with the women as they sang and danced and the full moon rose overhead. The night was very still; the smoke from twenty smouldering fires swirled about the ghostly group of dancers, a spurt of firelight revealing a sudden smile, a flash of eyes, the silhouette of a swaying figure. For hours the rhythm pulsed on like a heartbeat from the land, linking every living creature in ritual union. Then someone noticed the eerie dullness of the moon, its dark-red, bloodstained glow. Whispers rippled uneasily through the crowd. The women froze, the singing stopped, the ritual link was shattered. The moon in eclipse was an evil omen, a herald of chaos and death. The company scattered in a confusion of bodies and blankets as we fled with our children back to our camps.

Sunrise dispelled the immediate fear, but anxiety and tension lingered like the early-morning mist until the final phase of the ceremony had been completed. While many voiced the traditional belief that the eclipse was a portend of death, danger or disaster, others interpreted it as a demonstration of Jackie Wunawun's power.

We talked to Wunawun later and asked him how he knew there was to be an eclipse. His eyes twinkled under the brim of his panama as he shook his head emphatically. 'I tell you,' he said, 'that was a very special moon.' Whether he had known or not, one thing was for sure: no one was going to forget Jackie Wunawun's Kunapippi.

George Milpurrur, his wife Nancy and three of
their children, Graham, baby George and Shirley,
camp beside the Glyde River during a hunting
expedition.

1979

We returned to Arnhem Land again in June 1979, this time with an invitation from Milpurrur to camp with him and his family. We had first encountered Milpurrur at Murwangi cattle station in 1978, his legs sticking out from under his Toyota truck which was in its usual immobile state. He had emerged at last covered in grease, a fierce and powerful man whose contempt for us was plain. During the following month he had permitted us to spend an occasional day with him when he was painting a bark or rounding up cattle on the Arafura plains, but this time we were invited to stay.

Milpurrur was then about forty-two and the leader of the Ganalbingu clan. The Ganalbingu is a small and self-sufficient group who have defiantly clung to the traditional way of life. Milpurrur is not a person to be trifled with: his anger and ferocity are widely feared, but he is much respected for his powers of healing and his deep knowledge of an adherence to the *Madayin*.

When we arrived at his camp, Milpurrur was sitting in his bough shade cutting long strips of discarded linoleum that he had salvaged from the settlement dump. His eight-month-old son George was cradled in his lap as he worked. 'What are you making, Wawa?' I asked. Milpurrur grinned. 'You'll see tomorrow,' he said. He selected a site for us to camp close to his own, then disappeared into the bush with an axe, returning ten minutes later dragging two tall trees. He cut and erected the poles and helped us gather branches for our huge bough shade. His wife Nancy and the children brought firewood and we all sat down to a camp-warming celebration of tea and biscuits.

There was never an idle moment at Milpurrur's camp. If he was not making tools, utensils, spears or ceremonial items he would be painting a bark or carving and decorating large totemic creatures for sale to art and craft outlets. By the following morning six of the linoleum strips had been transformed, bound in bush string and spun with orange parrot feathers. By the end of the week they had become ceremonial belts hung with elaborate tassels of parrot feathers and white goose down.

During the following month we were taken on hunting, fishing and food gathering expeditions and on searches for raw ochre, bark and trees for carving. As my skin brother, Milpurrur assumed a protective brotherly role. Despite his earlier reluctance to be photographed he was now going out of his way to show us things of interest and teach us about his culture. We were proudly introduced to his clan country and led obliquely into Aboriginal custom and law. In everything we did there were lessons to be learned, techniques and skills to be acquired. Nancy and the children always accompanied Milpurrur on these expeditions. While he took the boys to hunt, she would hoist baby George in a sling on her back and three-year-old Shirley on her shoulder and go in search of sugar-bag or turtles' eggs, always making sure a fire was ready for the hunters' return. The group was strong and mutually supportive and Milpurrur, the fearsome hunter-warrior, was a remarkable family man, frequently playful and loving with his children.

The dry season that year was especially dry: a short wet season followed by unusually hot winds had baked the ground and by August the bush was parched. One day when we were out in the Toyota with all the family, Milpurrur suddenly directed us to turn off the track. For an hour he guided us at walking pace through dense bush and brittle scrub, snaking in and out of trees and over logs, dead branches falling in our wake. Suddenly we were forced to halt: before us was a rift valley some fifteen metres deep, a tropical oasis of rocks, springs and thick vegetation. 'This is my granny's country,' said Milpurrur, leading us down into the jungle. Through walls of grass and spiky pandanus we made our way in single file towards the rocks and the cool, dripping caverns. Stopping inside a cave Milpurrur pointed with his *bunduk* (spear thrower) to the rock above our heads. Slowly our eyes grew accustomed to the darkness. Pointing out the faded lines of a painting, he explained. 'These ones here,' he said, tapping the rock, 'these are milpurrurs, flying foxes. My namesake, my Dreaming.' He told us how as a boy he had camped here with his father when they were trying to avoid contact with Balanda.

Out in the sun again he led us through a jungle of

palms, vines and flowering bushes, a sumptuous secret garden vibrant with the sounds and songs of life. We stopped beside a tiny pool. 'Try this one, it's like fridge water,' laughed Milpurrur pointing to the spring that fed the pool. 'It never stops,' he said, 'even in a drought there's always water here.' He showed us the traditional way to gather and carry water in strips of resinous paperbark and how to make fire using nothing but sticks. 'This place, Mudjawakalal,' he said, with a sweeping look that embraced the surrounding rocks and jungle, 'is a special dreaming place for us Ganalbingu people.'

Water a shrine, fire an implement. Of the four natural elements—earth, air, fire and water—fire is the only one used exclusively by humans. For the Aborigines fire has many purposes, but it is the only tool they use for management of the land; as hunter-gatherers they have never tilled the land, but have controlled it with fire. Burning off is used not only to protect a camp from the possibility of bushfire, but also to 'clean' the country and ensure that hunting grounds do not become too dense and impenetrable.

A few days later a demonstration of this skill took us by surprise. We were on our way to Gartji to go fishing when Milpurrur ordered Clive to stop the vehicle. He and the boys jumped out, indicating that I should come with them while Clive drove on to Gartji with Nancy and the smaller children. No sooner were we out of the truck than the boys were brandishing fire-sticks made of rolled bark fibre. They lit the grass beneath our feet and within seconds, as I raced ahead of them photographing furiously, a wall of fire leapt up, cutting us off from the track. The boys fanned out, lighting the dry grass, while the wind behind us spread the blaze. After ten minutes an enormous arc of flame was advancing on us at an alarming speed. The heat was intense, but I noticed with some relief, ahead of us dense pandanus and tropical jungle indicated the possibility of water or a swamp.

I followed closely in Milpurrur's footsteps as black smoke full of charred litter engulfed us. He turned and laughed: 'Don't worry, Yappa,' he chided, 'this one is a good fire.' I stumbled through the rainforest, trying to keep up as my cameras caught on vines and pandanus ripped my legs. 'Good time for catching goanna,' said Milpurrur and as we plunged into the creek one shot past us, instantly pursued by the boys with shouts and spears. Milpurrur waited for

them to catch the metre-long monster and then, with the pandanus along one side of the creek exploding into flame, he set the opposite bank alight.

The fire roared on both sides of us as we filed thigh-deep along the narrow creek bed and finally out into a wider swamp, one side of which had already been razed. On we went through the blackened smouldering bush. I realized my feet were boiling in my boots, but incredibly my barefoot companions seemed impervious to the heat! An ibis was speared and a wallaby shot before we reached Garji billabong where Clive, Nancy, Ben and the children waited. From the bank we watched in safety as the raging beauty of the fire roared towards us from the other side of the water. Flames leapt six or seven metres into the air, blinding waves of smoke left us gasping; but the billabong stopped the the fire, precisely as Milpurrur had intended. As a demonstration of how the elements could be harnessed it was an awesome performance.

On other expeditions Milpurrur explained about Aboriginal medicine and pointed out the numerous herbs, leaves and insects that are used for medicinal purposes. One day when I had a cold we collected a handful of green ants and put them in a tin. 'Squash them all up in cold water,' said Milpurrur directing the process. 'This one will fix you up, Bulandjan.' Nancy watched with amusement as I gingerly sipped the revolting brew. It was bitter and presumably full of formic acid, but my cold didn't get any worse. Milpurrur also described concoctions for headache, stomach ache, scorpion bites and sores. For every ailment he seemed to know a remedy.

One day Ben was struck with fever and a violent rash. Throughout the day I struggled to cool him down but his temperature continued to rise and by late that night I had become alarmed. Everyone had turned in early after a long day's hunting and only the dogs were still awake, busily scavenging around the camp. Ben lay semi-delirious under the mosquito net, his fever raging and his body blotched with rash. No amount of cold compresses would bring his temperature down. Exhausted and sick with worry, I suddenly thought of Milpurrur. 'You can't go now,' Clive said, 'he'll be asleep.' Then he looked at Ben again. 'I'll go,' he said and disappeared into the darkness.

Some minutes later he returned with Milpurrur and an excited group of children. Milpurrur subdued them with a

George Milpurrur used traditional Aboriginal techniques and medicine to cure Ben's raging fever.

gesture and slipped inside the mosquito-net with Ben. The children huddled in the shadows. Milpurrur dipped his fingers in a bowl of water, shook them, passed them through his hair, then placed his strong black hands on the small white body. Ben lay motionless on his side, the focus of all our attention. Slowly and carefully Milpurrur felt his way up Ben's spine, stroking his body and feeling for the internal organs. Rhythmically massaging and exploring, he ran his hands through his hair or across his shoulders and back to Ben, his eyes never leaving the child's passive face, as he drew the heat from the small body and replaced it with power from his own. He ran his fingers through his armpits and placed them firmly on Ben's temples, pressing and squeezing round his head. Ben woke and stared at the intruder. Milpurrur smiled, encouraging his young patient to stay still. Ben did not flinch under the pressure of those strong hands, nor when Milpurrur blew hard and loud on to his back and chest. His eyes cleared and his gaze locked with Milpurrur's. After ten minutes of this firm massage the treatment stopped and Milpurrur declared there was nothing seriously wrong. 'That rash will soon go,' he pronounced, 'that fever tomorrow.' As he spoke Ben sat up and brushing aside the net as if nothing had been wrong, joined the other children. Soon he was playing with the kids around the campfire. Milpurrur smiled and lit himself a cigarette.

One night in September Clive and Milpurrur returned from 'men's business' in some excitement. A Kunapippi ceremony near Maningrida was into its final phase and the climax was to take place over the next full moon. As respected leader of the Ganalbingu clan, Milpurrur, should be there with his relations to participate.

Next day complex preparations had to be made. Who should go? How many could we take in our vehicle? How long would we be away? It was eventually decided that Clive, Ben and I, Milpurrur, his brother Jilman, several other male relatives and his sons would go. The women and smaller children would stay behind. Swags, spears, ceremonial gear, jerry cans of water, cooking pots and sacks of flour were piled on to the Toyota and in the late afternoon we set off.

We sped through the bush in growing excitement and anticipation, but a sudden impulse for solitude overwhelmed me. Without Nancy and the other women I did not want to play camp follower to this exclusively male experience. On reaching the Blythe River I asked to be left there with Ben: we would camp there until the men returned from the ceremony. My scheme was met with indignation and alarm: alone in the bush, hours from anywhere, without a vehicle, without a two-way radio? What if somebody came, what about buffalo, what about snakes? But I insisted. I needed a few days' rest—a fact they couldn't deny.

We had stopped here several times before. An oasis in the surrounding bushland, it was an idyllic place to fish and swim. The river's wet-season course, 200 metres across, was now, late in the dry season, a bare landscape of rocks, roots and sandbars; one solitary tree on a sandbar provided a perfect camp site thirty metres from the water.

We forded the river and turned off the track to our favourite spot. Darkness was falling as everyone tumbled out of the cramped vehicle; hastily I gathered up sleeping bags, mosquito net, billy, books, cameras and enough food for several days. Milpurrur helped me rig the net from the gnarled, leaning tree. 'If buffalo come,' he said, 'you climb this tree, Yappa.' He was serious and showed me the best way up. Shaking his head with incomprehension he said, 'It's no good you and Wamut alone in the bush, too much danger. You make a big fire and keep those buffalo away.'

The ceremony ground was still two hours away and shouting goodbye, the men and boys piled into the truck. I picked Ben up and was heading back to my camp when out of the dusk came Milpurrur, carrying his gun. 'Yappa, you take this, you may need it,' he said, but I refused, explaining that I'd been in more dangerous situations before and didn't believe in having a gun. 'Wawa,' I told him, 'you need it for hunting, you keep it.' 'Okay,' shrugged Milpurrur, 'but you burn a fire all night, Bulandjan.' And he bade us a final farewell: '*Bo bo, tchu tchutna.*'

The vehicle lurched back on to the track, its noise soon consumed by the clatter of crickets and the busy nightlife of the bush. In the dark Ben and I surveyed our camp spot and our few possessions piled under the tree. I laid out a blanket for him and took a long deep breath of the warm night air. From our sandy position on the bank we looked out across the tree-lined river where high among the melaleucas the moon was slowly rising. For a full moon it seemed uncommonly dark and dull.

Aboriginal taboos prohibit staring at the moon and many stories depict it as a powerful and mysterious force associated with pregnancy and death. Now I remembered Malangi's story, told to us one night as we sat in his camp by the moonlight: 'The moon was a selfish and greedy man who was jealous of his sons. He had tried to drown them in a fish trap. His wives had found their sons and had chased after the man to try and kill him. The man ran up a tree for safety but the women set light to it so he fled into the sky. As he vanished he swore they could not kill him. So each month he vanishes only to be reborn.'

I continued to stare, my eyes locked into that dark moon as, slowly, it revealed itself between the branches. 'Funny moon, Mummy,' said Ben. 'You're right,' I said, realizing we were witnessing an eclipse. Remembering last year at Mowemba I shivered. In an effort to shake off my apprehension I leapt into action. A fire had to be lit and Ben's supper prepared, but when I grabbed the torch it wouldn't work. I rushed blindly into the gloom, stumbling over rocks and roots in my search for firewood, but there was none nearby. I was suddenly overcome with fear, not for myself but for Ben. I could not leave him alone in the dark while I went further away. There was a huge fallen tree nearby. Without stopping to think I threw all my strength at it to drag it to our camp. A snake shot out between my feet. I froze, shocked by my own stupidity. If something happened to me, Ben was helpless; alone he would perish. Somehow I got a grip of myself, and the tree, and managed to drag it the fifty metres to our camp.

Together we built a great fire. But where were the matches? They weren't in my bag or my pockets. I tipped out our food box, rummaged among my cameras. Not a match to be found. I didn't dare look at the moon; I could feel its cold creeping up my spine. Aboriginal methods of making a fire flashed through my mind, but twenty minutes with Milpurrur one afternoon had produced little more than a wisp of smoke, blistered hands and aching wrists. I had even forgotten to ask him what special wood he had used. What to do? Milpurrur's words raced in my brain: 'Make *big* fire.' Perhaps the matches had fallen out as we unloaded from the Toyota. I darted in that direction and accidently kicked the torch. It flickered for an instant on the ground, exposing a throwaway lighter half-buried in the sand. I pounced on it unbelievingly, but the sceptic in me already knew it was probably useless. Willing it to work,

I flicked it with my thumb. The flint flashed but did not light. I tried again, wishing we had some petrol that might catch the spark. Nothing. I shook it fiercely, and tried once more. Amazingly it lit and soon we had a blazing fire and enough light to see by. I gathered wood to last the night, made soup and organized our camp.

The darkness closed in. It was strangely silent now. Not a cricket rattled. I strained my ears for the soothing slap of the river running on the rocks. Not a murmur. Not a ripple. Had even the river stopped in its tracks? The moon was being consumed by the earth's shadow and its blood-red face stared blankly at us in the stillness while round its rim a faint blue tinge appeared. Damp cold rose from the river and the world was deathly quiet. Then I thought I heard the wind: the air was still, but I could hear something clearly, a rushing wind approaching. Suddenly the darkness exploded into a mass of flapping wings. Birds! Thousands of giant birds, blundering, screeching, tumbling all round and into us. A silhouette crossed the moon—not birds but flying foxes! No evil omen but Milpurrur's namesakes, Milpurrur's totem, come to keep us company. We laughed and called to them and joined them in their chatter. For minutes they swooped and swirled, almost blundering into us with their enormous wings. Then like a great black wave they launched themselves upon our tree, slithering and sliding on the sagging branches, chattering and swearing at each other as they fell and floundered in the dark. Ben and I laughed and laughed in delighted relief.

The world had not stopped. A small sliver of moon was shining bright and the night was coming alive again. Crickets chirped and Muk-muk, the night owl, called to his mate along the river, whose softly slapping rhythm I could hear again.

For the rest of the night I lay on the sand close to the fire following the moon's progress to resume its brilliant self and thought about the ceremony somewhere to the west, where hundreds of men would be singing and dancing their way through the rites of the sacred Kunapippi. Or would they? How were they interpreting this moon? But it didn't really matter: here beside the Blythe I celebrated my own ceremony of revelation and liberation.

Throughout the night the flying foxes were a source of company and delight. Hanging upside down from every branch they resembled a mass of black drapes. Once, when a crocodile barked close by, the whole tree took off whirling and shrieking alarm and reminded me to stoke up the fire. From time to time as I put on more wood, their red eyes would glint in the light; or one would lose its grip on the overloaded branch and slip, sweeping several others with it as it fell, so that the tree became a squawking, fluttering mass of indignation.

The moon began to sink and the sky to lighten. The flying foxes feasted on the flowers of the tree. Grey, green, mauve, pink, the pre-dawn colours spread brilliantly across the sky; the flying foxes undraped themselves from the branches, whirled through a final aerial dance and disappeared as suddenly as they had come.

For two peaceful days Ben and I explored the Blythe. We splashed and swam in the deeper pools—a trifle wary of cruising crocodiles—followed ants on their march for miles, and solved the mystery of the river that had stopped in its tracks. The Blythe is tidal and when the current meets the incoming tide the river stands still at high-water mark for a full fifteen minutes. The forces of nature are locked in combat until the tide retreats and the river flows on again—all because of the power of the moon.

Ultimately a rumbling of trucks disturbed the tranquil bush. The ceremony was over and the men returned. Exhausted, exhilarated, covered in dust, caked in red ochre or flaking white clay, they swarmed off the vehicles and into the river with whoops of glee. Burralang—Clive—was with them, an honorary Yolngu, a man among men, ordering tea to impress his friends. The billy was boiled and the hungry mob demolished the remaining rations. 'Okay this camp?' Milpurrur asked with a quizzical look. 'Terrific, Wawa,' I replied. Did he know about the flying foxes I wondered. The ceremony had been a great success, it seemed, but being a sacred ceremony no one could elaborate.

There was little time to rest, however, as important business awaited us at Nangalala near Ramangining. Five boys were to be initiated, three of them sons of Djoma, a clan elder, and the other two their cousins. All were nephews of Bulain, Balang and Malangi, brothers of Binalany and related to Milpurrur through a complex connection on their mothers' side. Thus the coming circumcision rite was an important event for the clans of the region. To our surprise and joy we learned that Djoma, Bulain and the other elders had conferred and decided both to invite us to the ceremony and to allow us to record it.

We arrived at Nangalala in mid-afternoon. Beneath the shade of a banyan tree the populations of Ramanging and Nangalala had gathered to witness and participate in a Bungaling-Bungaling, a joyous public celebration of the birth of an important man's first child. A lock of the child's hair had been sent with relations from Rembarnga country.

Painted bodies whirled and stamped, twisted and leapt, as clap-sticks vigorously accompanied the songs. The air was vibrant with dust and dancers. Slapping of thighs, chanting and the drone of the didgeridoo accompanied the stamping feet. Feathered waistbands swirled in the sunlight. Shining bodies adorned with ochre and clay were paintings come alive. Milpurrur tucked his packet of Marlboro into his belt of orange parrot feathers and joined the younger men to perform a spectacular dance of leaps and spins. The crowd applauded with delight and the boys competed in a frenzy to outdo each other's speed and skill. The dust and dancers flew, and the didgeridoo went from man to man to sustain the pace.

As the sun began to set the tempo calmed. Led by the song-man the procession of dancers left the banyan tree for the open ceremony ground where, for the next eight days, the initiation would take place. Joined by all the initiated men, the dancers assembled in an all-male group. The women formed a ring around them, singing and chanting continuously as they circled the men. Djoma arrived escorting the five young boys and the chanting abruptly became a lament.

Gundbarra touched me on the arm to explain. 'The boys are leaving their mothers now, leaving as children; when they come back they will be men.' Tears poured down her cheeks, tears of pride, of loss, of ritual anguish. She had been through it all before with her own sons. Every Aboriginal woman is a mother; if not literally then through her status as a skin mother to her skin sons and daughters.

In Arnhem Land initiation marks the first step towards manhood and the introduction to the *Madayin*. Until this time young boys live with their families and are brought up predominantly by women. Once circumcised the boys will theoretically live apart in camps supervised by young men, segregated from their female peers until they marry. Today, however, European ways and the need for schooling have broken down this strict segregation. Every boy must pass through initiation to become a full tribal man, but the ceremonies do more than simply provide the occasion for

During an initiation ceremony at Nangalala in 1979, male relatives of the initiates were decorated with white clay for their part in the week-long ceremony. Two of the dancers show Ben a polaroid of themselves.

Djoma (centre) was host for the initiation ceremony at Nagalala in 1979. The initiates—three of his sons and two of his nephews—sit with him among the other elders to observe and learn as the songs and dances are performed. This Gurrmulkuma ceremony literally means 'making men' and ritualizes the boys' introduction into the complexities of tribal law.

circumcision, for the making of men: they also link the present with past by recreating the events of the Dreaming and restating the instructions of the totemic ancestors, thus reaffirming the creation of Aboriginal society and explaining its long-established laws and customs.

The boys, aged between nine and thirteen, looked innocent and vulnerable with their long hair and delicate features. They were led in to sit uneasily among their elders. The quiet chanting continued after dark and the women returned to their families lamenting their loss. Later the boys retired with their *mungapuwuy*—their mothers' brothers, who were to act as their guardians throughout the initiation.

Each day for seven days the boys sat with the men, absorbing the cycle of songs and chants, listening and learning. In the late afternoon they moved to the ceremony ground where spectators gathered. The singing increased in rhythmic intensity. Dancers emerged from the bush like waves pounding upon a shore to perform their stylized dances based on clan motifs and totems, depicting perhaps a darting fish, a hungry bird, a butterfly in flight.

Malangi, Bulain and Gundbarra took it upon themselves to try and teach me: 'There, that one is that little fish again,' or 'This is about butterfly, you remember.' I could not, but watching fascinated and intrigued I could just distinguish the representation of a dingo from that of a brolga. Then the tempo changed and the women began to wail again, circling the men and proclaiming their pain. At a death ceremony we had witnessed some months before I had suddenly realised the significance of ritualising grief. Here again the women were publicly sharing their loss, giving their grief its fullest expression and finding a catharsis we in European society have denied ourselves.

For nearly a week the process continued daily, the routine changing only slightly but the number of participants and the intensity of their activity mounting steadily. Each day more relatives arrived, including important men from the boys' mothers' family, keepers of songs and dances without whom the ceremony could not continue.

Malangi and Bulain had set up camp with their families around the ceremony ground, along with the visitors from Milingimbi and Dippirringur. Malangi's wife Gundbarra took charge of Ben, he romped around her camp with Muykul, May and the other children.

On the seventh day things took a different turn. Faint singing began with the first light of dawn and by sun-up the dancers were blinding in their whiteness, freshly covered in liquid clay; agile apparitions, superhuman and ghostly, they joked and frolicked around the camp. The five boys huddled wearily together in their blankets, bemused with anticipation and fear. The seven days away from their peers in this strange adult camp were beginning to tell—from time to time the boys took refuge in well-thumbed comic books.

As the sun rose the chanting and the tension increased. Young men leapt about with spears and whoops of delight. The women covered themselves in ochre and about midday began to wail, circling the men and boys in a ritual display of emotion that was part longing for their sons, part sorrow at their loss, part pride in their future men. The boys were escorted out of the camp and into the shady courtyard of a former mission house where Djoma, Bulain, Balang and a dozen male relatives awaited them. In the deep shade of the banana palms mattresses and blankets had been laid out, billies of tea prepared and ochre freshly ground. The elders had already discussed my role in the imminent all-male body-painting ritual and consented to my presence as observer and recorder.

Bulain, uncle to the boys and a senior elder of the Gupapuyngu clan, sat solid as a stone. His role in this important section of the ceremony was to sing the painting on to the bodies of the boys. He would sing the songs from his Dreaming—sugar-bag, or wild honey, an important Dreaming that belonged also to his nephews and would adorn their bodies. Balang was mixing ochre on a large stone palette while Malangi, another uncle to the boys, elder of the Liagalawumirri clan and a guardian of these rites, hovered in the background smoking a long pipe and keeping a watchful eye on the proceedings. Djoma, father of Junganju, Madawilli and Baymumgimbi, aged nine, eleven and thirteen, was host for the ceremony.

Some gentle jokes were cracked, a bowl of evil-looking glue extracted from the roots of orchids appeared and the serious business of body painting began. Bulain set the tone with his gentle song. Bulang, silver-haired and wise, began to paint—not on bark this time, but on the body of his nephew. With meticulous loving brushstrokes he prepared the boy for his entry into manhood just as he himself had been prepared, and his father and his father's father before him.

The boys lay still for hours, only their eyes moving as their guardians worked intently over them, outlining on their skin their clan design, the figures of their totemic ancestors and the stories of their country. The penetrating rhythm of the sticks and the low chanting of the ancient songs seemed to pulse from the earth itself, merging with the swaying rhythm of the paint being transferred from palette to body as the subtle lines and crosshatching began to weave a suit of intricate mesh and brilliant colour on the bodies of the boys.

During pauses for tea the boys rose stiffly to admire each other's totemic clothing. By late afternoon their regalia was complete with armbands of ochred string and orange parrot feathers. Around their heads and waists huge turbans and belts of feathered bush string were tied, each one a work of art made specially for each boy. In awe the initiates were led to the ceremony ground to sit with their fathers and elders for their last night of boyhood.

Malangi, looking now like commanding officer, his pipe held behind his back like a swagger stick, came strutting up to us to declare proudly, 'Proper ceremony this one, we make young men proper Yolngu way.' Circumcision, he said would bring good fortune to the families of the brave, but dishonour to the boy whose screams were heard. Everyone was obviously very proud of this ceremony and willing it to go well as they gathered to share the night of dancing and song that would continue until dawn. The boys slept briefly in their paint while the song-men kept vigil, chanting the final songs in the cycle that must be completed before the circumcision can take place.

At dawn, tired and apprehensive, the boys are wrapped in cotton sheets and led into the bush for a final face-painting. White clay, ground and chewed is blown from the mouth in a fine spray, again and again until their faces and hair are gleaming white, then they are taken back to the camp to await the next bewildering assault. At the ceremony ground the crowd reassembles. Grass palliasses are laid out to receive the boys. Women chant and wail, circling continuously. Half crouching, dancers white with clay steal out of the bush, like wary dingoes checking out the site. Wide-eyed and dazed, the boys sit close and wait.

Subtly the tempo changes. Tension mounts. A command is given and the camp erupts in a clatter of spears, a pounding of feet, a pall of dust. The boys are surrounded by a seething, stamping mass of men, brandishing spears, hissing and whooping. Then up, up, the boys are gently lifted on to the shoulders of their *mungapuwuy*, their heads held down so that they see nothing.

The procession snakes out of the bush towards the ceremony ground amid a crescendo of chanting, clapping, hissing, wailing and bloodcurdling dramatics. It enters the expectant crowd and the boys are lowered and vanish from sight. The men close in, surrounding and protecting their proteges for the climax, while the women wail and flagellate themselves to drown out the cries of pain. Every man, woman and youth is united in ceremonial frenzy.

Abruptly the chanting stops. The rites have been accomplished. The collective mass sobs with relief as the initiates vanish, silently whisked by their guardians into the cool, embracing bush.

A burst of humorous dances breaks the spell. There is laughter and chatter, speeches of thanks, applause, gifts for the dancers and congratulations all round. The women, their ritual role fulfilled, the task of 'growing up' the boys now completed, will return to their families and to the nurturing of their children, their community and their culture.

Meanwhile in the bush the ceremony continues. Tenderness and time-tried tribal medicine will salve the young men's wounds. Profound and gentle words will impart the tribal law. Men now among men, the initiates embark on their long journey into wisdom and knowledge.

The dust had barely settled on the ceremony ground when it was stirred up again by the arrival of a helicopter, the first ever seen at Nangalala. The children gathered round with curiosity to wave as Malangi, Dhartangu and Binalany accompanied by two government officials took off to survey the swamps and river estuary. Their mission, to chart clan country and to locate and record the illegal netting in Aboriginal waters by an Australian syndicate of barramundi fishing boats. For Arnhem Land, inaccessible though it may appear to be, is never without threat of one sort of invasion or another.

'The sun is a woman who travels the world spread-
ing warmth and light.'

From sunrise to sunset the Aboriginal mythological ancestors travelled the land creating its features and its form.

Rock paintings throughout Arnhem Land depict
the nature of the flora and fauna and the exploits
of the Dreamtime ancestors and supernatural
spirits. They also illustrate significant events
(*above*). At Nangalour a giant figure of a white
man is superimposed on earlier rock paintings.

Mimi spirits were traditionally painted on rock in blood. These carved and decorated Mimi figures made at Mormega outstation will be sold as craft items.

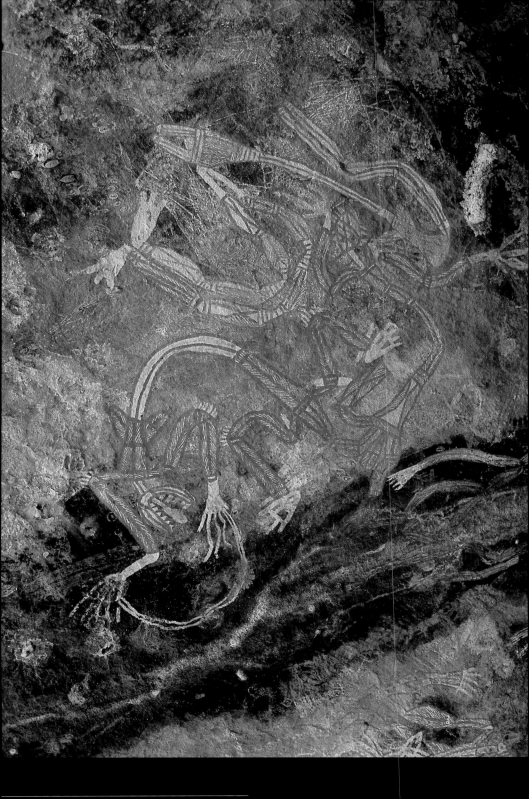

Female Namarakain spirits at Sorcery Rock in
western Arnhem Land.

The land is the essence of Aboriginal people
themselves. The land is their heritage, from it
stems their religion and law and within it a continuity of past and present has been maintained
for more than 40,000 years.

A quartz-like rock found in Rembarnga country has been the source of essential stone-age tools for thousands of years. These spearheads and blades have been traded throughout northern and central

The transmission of knowledge (and information) is an integral part of Aboriginal culture. Mil-purrur explains to his sons the rock paintings at Mudjawakalal.

Opposite: In Arnhem Land the semi-tropical swamps and plains provide an abundance of bush foods and game. From the earliest age all children are taught to gather bush tucker for themselves.

Beside the Cadell River young men from a nearby outstation practise their skills with the didgeridoo and clap-sticks. Learning clan songs is an important part of their education.

More than 3,000 Aborigines in Arnhem Land have left the settlements and missions to return to their clan country or homelands to set up family camps. These homeland centres are known by whites as 'outstations'.

While most of the Aborigines living on reserves in other parts of Australia have no security of ten- ure, the Aborigines in Arnhem Land hold title to their land under an Act of Parliament. Although Arnhem Land may never be sold, exploitation of the land by mining and development remains a constant threat.

At Kalobidada outstation traditional bark huts made of stringy bark (*Eucalyptus tetradonta*) provide an appropriate cool, simple and inexpensive form of shelter.

Overleaf: Shelter at Kalobidada ranged from simple bark shades to enclosed bark huts and the platform version used by Mandarg and his family. The platform hut is cooler in the dry season and drier in the wet season. An additional advantage is that smouldering logs kindled beneath the platform help eliminate at least some of the mosquitoes.

Mandarg's daughter Becky with baby Vicky who was named after the European midwife. All Aboriginal people in Arnhem Land have their own Aboriginal names but Western bureaucracy and the missions have demanded that they be prefixed with a Christian or European name for the simpli fication of official records. Thus some people were known by their Aboriginal name while others introduced themselves by their European name.

Milpurrur, an elder of the Ganalbingu clan, works as a stockman for several months each year but adheres closely to traditional customs and law. An extremely skilled painter and craftsman he is shown *above* making the hook of a bunduk (spear

The semi-nomadic lifestyle follows the seasons. In the wet season good shelter is important but during the dry season access to water, hunting grounds and ceremonies demand mobility. Mil-purrur and Nancy pack up camp to move on.

Overleaf: Malangi of the Liagalawumirri clan smokes the long 'traditional' pipe which was introduced into Arnhem Land by the Maccassan several centuries ago. Nellie, wife of Bulun Bulun, smokes a modern briar.

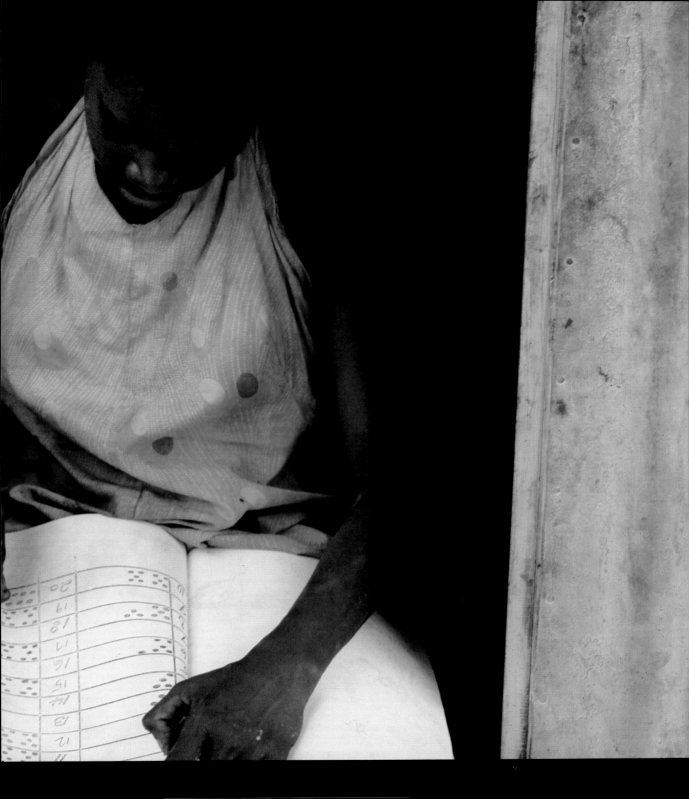

Education in Arnhem Land is primarily in English, each settlement providing a school for children up to seventh grade. Outstation schools are less formally organized by the community itself and are supervised once a fortnight by a visiting European teacher.

At Mormega outstation, schoolwork may seem irrelevant but is sometimes necessary.

Outside the range of Darwin radio or newspapers, Arnhem Land is cut off from most external information. At Kalobidada Mandarg's son, Jackie, had a radio with a 30-metre aerial, and provided us with the first news we had heard for a month . . . from Singapore!

At Marpi Bulain paints sugar-bag dreaming. In 1979 one sixth of the income in Arnhem Land came from the sale of art and craft.

Opposite: Graham watches intently as his father Milpurrur paints a bark relating to his clan country and his deceased relatives.

Most outstations have either a four-wheel-drive vehicle, boat or like Wunawun at Mowemba, a tractor.

Gathering 'sugar-bag' or wild honey is considered to be women's business and can be hard work. First the nest has to be located. This is often in the hollowed-out branch of a tree, but keen eyesight is needed as the insects which make the honey are smaller than a normal fly. Once found the tree is felled to reach the honey which often produces no

Overleaf: After a mining survey team illegally entered Arnhem Land to lay seismic lines through a sacred site local traditional owners set up a road block on the Arnhem Highway. The Chief Minister of the Northern Territory ultimately apologized.

The family is a strong entity and on outstations the men also play an important part in raising the children.

Top: A new arrival is welcomed by older brothers and sisters.
Above: Despite the lack of roads, bikes are a status symbol amongst the children.

Graham.

Lilies are not only refreshing bush tucker but decoration also.

After a successful goanna hunt Milpurrur's boys hold up their catch to their mother who is waiting on the plain below.

Overleaf: Bulain carves up a magpie goose and shares it amongst his family.

Most outstations have a 12-volt two-way radio. At
Kalobidada Jimmy talks to Maningrida Outstation
Resource Centre.

In Arnhem Land, where water is plentiful, bathing is not so much a chore as a pleasurable pastime.

Searching for yabbies at Gartji billabong.

George Milpurrur (*above*) of the Ganalbingu clan and Bulain (*opposite*) of the Guparpingu clan have painting, medicine and skin names in common but are traditionally tribal rivals.

A bark painting by Bunungurr tells a traditional story but reflects the style of comic books which were the only reading matter we saw in Arnhem Land.

SITE OF SIGNIFICANCE

BEYOND THIS POINT LIES AN ABORIGINAL SITE OF A SACRED/DANGEROUS NATURE

UNDER SECTION 69 OF THE ABORIGINAL LAND
RIGHTS (NORTHERN TERRITORY) ACT 1976

TRESPASS ON A SACRED SITE CARRIES A PENALTY OF

$1,000

ONE THOUSAND DOLLARS.

BY REQUEST OF TRADITIONAL OWNERS

In 1978 a thousand Aborigines from northern Australia gathered at Groote Eylandt to
take part in a week-long festival of traditional song and dance organized by the
Aboriginal Cultural Foundation. Nandjiwarra Amagula, a tribal elder from Groote
Eylandt and the Chairman of the Foundation's Executive of tribal leaders explained
that the festival's objective was, 'to link the
chain between all tribal people, to reinforce
our culture and our kinship ties'. The festival
also created a forum in which to discuss the
threat of mining and development in the
region.

The didgeridoo or drone pipe is made from a branch hollowed out by white ants — termites. To play the 'doo requires a circular breathing technique while its tone is determined by its length and size. Sometimes the 'doo is painted or carved but in this case electrical tape provided decoration.

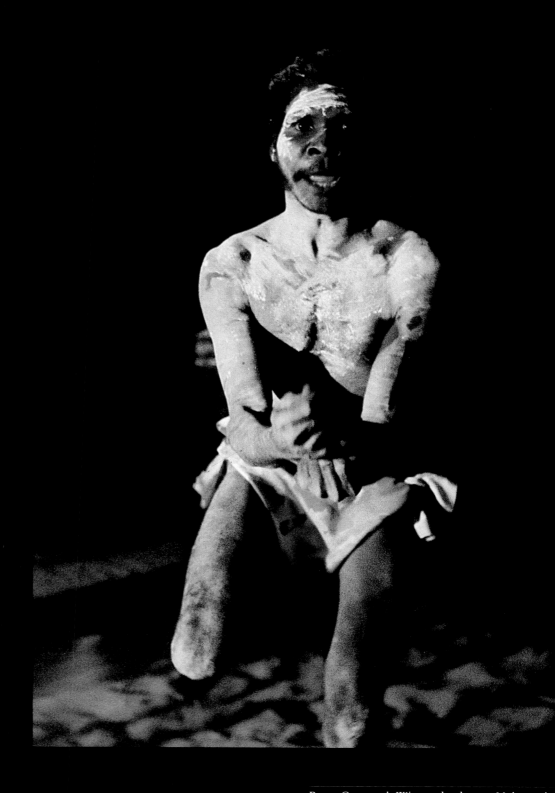

Peter Gurruwul Wirrpanda dances Mokuy, the
spirit of the dead.

Dancers from Groote Eylandt and Numbulwar use
flags to represent the arrival of the Maccassans in
their praus.

Dancers from the Yirrkala and Elcho region re-enact the Dhuwa spirits collecting sugar-bag. The feathered string represents the track (trail) of the honey ants to and from their nest.

Walter Jimilbina is employed to drive heavy
earth-moving equipment.

Milpurrur returns to Mudjawakalal with his children for a day of exploration and education in important Ganalbingu clan country.

Gathering bush tucker.

Overleaf: Bulain's children explore the delicacies of water lilies, every part of which is edible.

Pandanus palm grows profusely in the swampier
regions of Arnhem Land and is used for making
mats, baskets and fish traps.
Top: Rordji returns to Yatalemarra with pandanus for weaving.

Above and opposite: Baypungala strips the
pandanus fronds of their spiny outer layer in preparation for weaving.

Bush string spun from fine strands of wood fibre
is coloured by pounding with yellow and red
ochre.

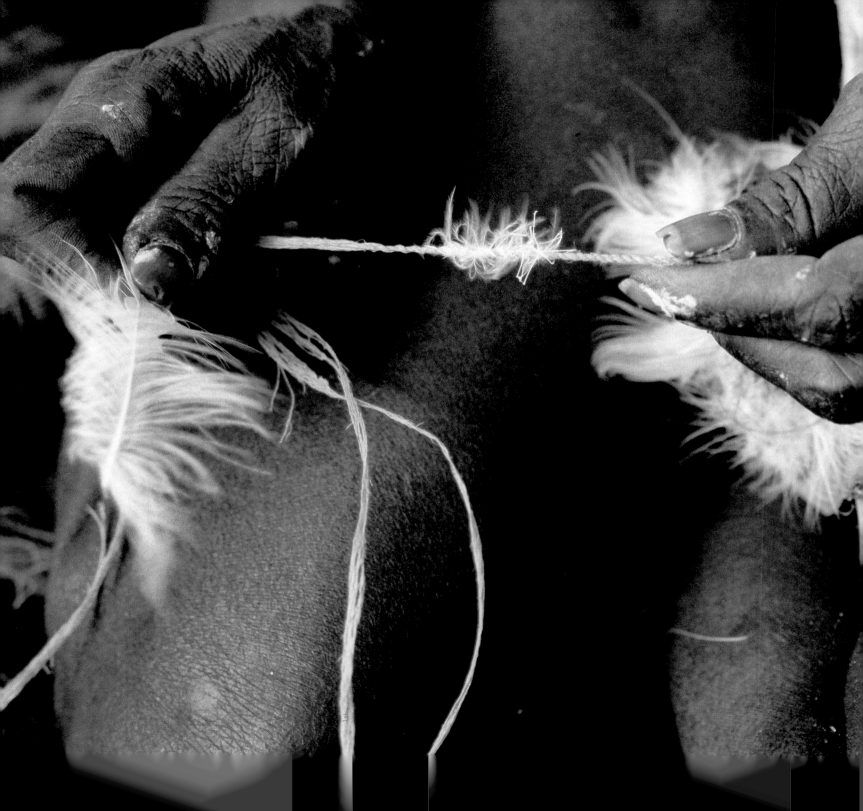

Pandanus is woven from the centre in close weave
to form mats, baskets and dilly bags.

Opposite: Baypungala weaving pandanus dilly bags.

A bark painting by Munyal depicts the use of a pandanus fish trap.

At Kopunga a traditional hollowed-out canoe,
now superseded by an aluminium dinghy, rests on
the sand dunes. Like many other outstations near

Pandanus kernels, clams, crabs, yam and a conch
boiling in the billy were offered for tea near
Kopunga . . .

Snails found in the roots of pandanus palm provide another source of protein and their shells can
be decorated for use as rattles during ceremonies.

Before the introduction of flour cycad nuts provided a source of carbohydrate, but first the nuts
had to be peeled then leached in running water
for five days before the pulp could be baked into
damper (unleavened bread).

Although hunting is traditionally men's business
the women often play an important role in assisting their husbands. Birpirri retrieves a magpie
goose shot by Bulain.

Traditionally, fire was the only land management
tool used by the Aborigines. Milpurrur and his
sons commence an annual burn-off to clean the
country of unnecessary undergrowth.

Burning-off provides an opportunity for hunting goanna which flee to the waterholes to escape the fire.

Opposite page, above: In burnt-off country Darrell, Peter and Frank quickly spot their prey. *Below:* A 'bunduk' is used to launch the spear which in this case is a three-pronged fish spear.

Frank admires Graham's goanna.

Shotguns are now as essential to survival as spears
were in the past.

The well-planned burn-off ends precisely as
Milpurrur intended at Gartji billabong which acts
as a fire-break.

After five hours' hunting Gurrmanamana returns with half a dozen geese.

Opposite: Milpurrur's sons Graham and Frank succeed in catching a wounded ibis.

Hunting is hard work but it's also fun especially
when the hunters are successful.

From the earliest age children learn about their environment. Girls and boys soon learn to identify bush foods and are taught to hunt and to gather bush tucker.

Overleaf: Milpurrur takes his sons hunting.

Goannas are plentiful in Arnhem Land. When cooked the meat is not unlike 'fishy chicken'. Milpurrur's children were delighted with their catch, though Ben was a little wary.

Overleaf: Bulain and seven of his eleven wives and some of his 52 children line up for a formal portrait after a successful hunting expedition.

Most bush vegetable foods, with the exception of
yams and cycad, are eaten raw, but fish and game
are roasted in hot ashes and served on fresh
paperbark or a bed of gum leaves. Nutritious deli-

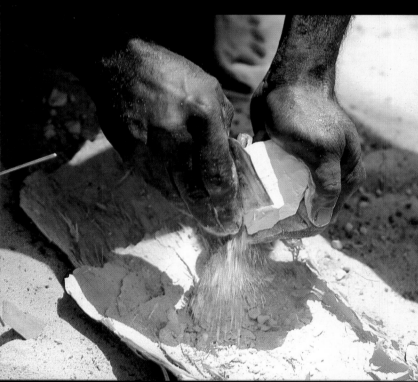

Painting on bark is a means of recording information and reaffirming the painter's relationship with his country and the stories of his ancestors. *Top left:* Bulun Bulun prepares a bark for painting. *Top right:* The bark is straightened using fire. *Above left:* Scraping white ochre into a fine powder. *Above right:* A handful of red ochre.

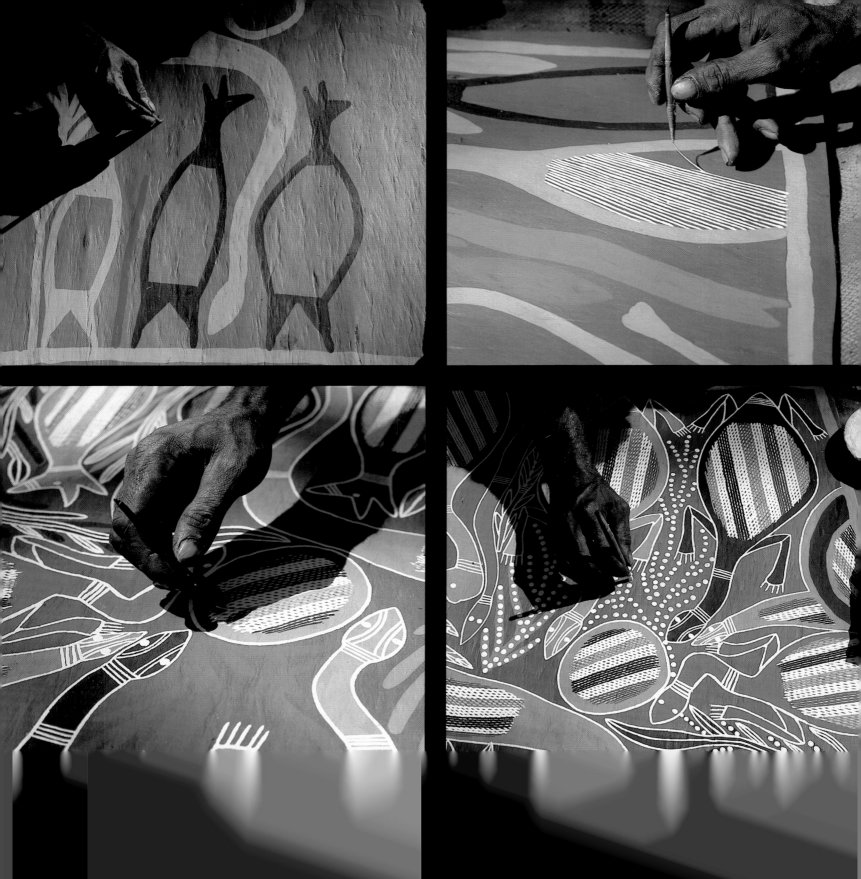

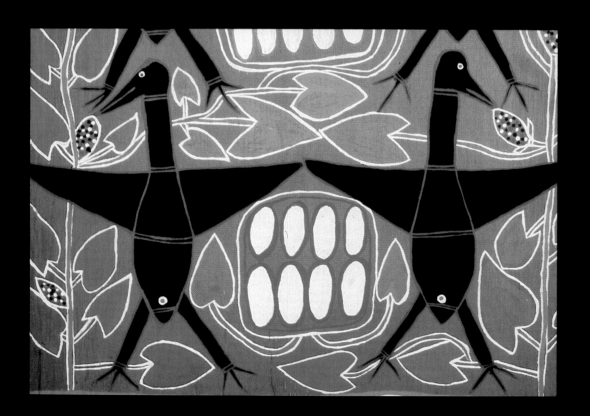

A bark painting by Yambal illustrates a legend
about the migratory black ibises which fly into
Arnhem Land pulling the rain clouds behind

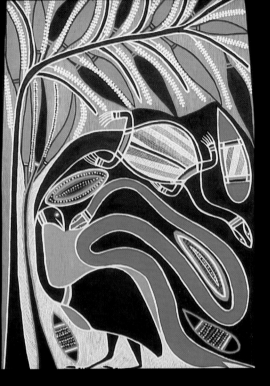

Bark paintings by Malangi (*top left*), Dhalyanda (*top right*) and Milpurrur (*above left*) illustrating their own clan totems and country. *Above right:* Malangi's painting describes the adventures of a Dreamtime ancestor, Gurrumuringu.

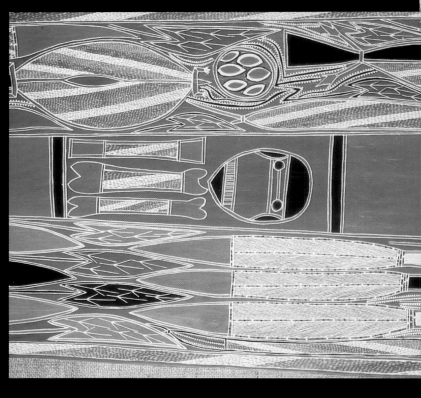

Bark paintings and details of barks by Milpurrur
(*top left*), Bulain (*top right*), Balang (*above left*)
and Bonapana (*above right*).

Bark paintings and details of barks by Dhartangu (*top left*), Bulain (*top right*), Bonapana (*above left*) and Gudhay Gudhay (*above right*).

Gubargu from Mormega in western Arnhem Land
with his painting of Mimi spirits.

At Nangalala in 1979 an initiation ceremony, 'Gurrmulkuma', was organized by Djoma to initiate five young boys into tribal law and 'make them young men'.

One of the elders is painted with white ochre — a form of chalk found locally.

Jungangu is painted with white ochre early in the ceremony. As the ceremony progresses the painting becomes increasingly more elaborate.

White body paint is used for its dramatic effect and also for protection from evil spirits. The armbands worn by the boys are made of bush string decorated with white ochre and orange parrot feathers.

A group of dancers prepared with white body
paint.

Overleaf: Throughout the ceremony the initiates remain with the songmen and the elders to observe, listen and learn.

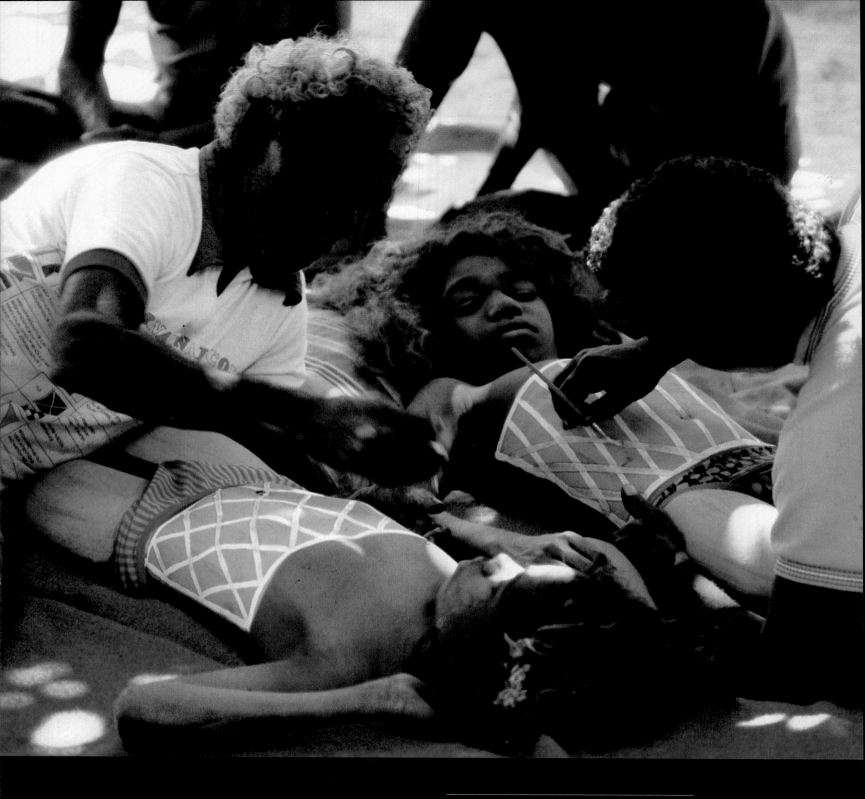

Body painting is an important ritual within a ritual; on the seventh day the initiates are meticulously painted with their appropriate clan design—sugar-bag dreaming.

On this final day of decoration the boys' faces are not painted but sprayed with colour. George sprays white from his mouth on to the face and hair of young Bulun Bulun.

Snaking out of the bush as the sun sets the young initiates are escorted to the ceremony ground by the dancers.

The initiates' totemic regalia is completed with
waistbands of feathered string, ochred armbands
and parrot-feather tassles made specially for each
boy. Instead of shorts they now wear 'nagas'.

Opposite: Young Bulun Bulun with his *mungapuwuy* or guardian, Warratjima, whose job it is to assist and care for his protégé throughout the initiation. *Above:* Younger brothers of the initiates are also painted for the ceremony.

Overleaf: The five initiates are now prepared for circumcision and initiation into tribal law.

The initiates are carried to the ceremony ground
to be 'made men'.

The 'open' part of the ceremony has ended. An elder carrying a sacred dilly bag watches as the boys are whisked away into the bush for further rites within the ritual and an intensive time of learning.

A successful ceremony completed, the dancers
perform before the elders for the last time.

An important time of learning follows initiation. Milpurrur spends time in the bush with his initiated son, Peter, teaching him tribal law.

'The moon was a jealous and cowardly man who
tried to kill his sons; but discovered by his wives
he fled up a tree. The women set light to the tree
and the man rose up into the night sky swearing
to return . . . after four days he came back again
as the moon.'

BIBLIOGRAPHY

Barwick, D. *Aboriginal and Islander History*. ANU Press, Canberra, 1979.

Bell, D. and Ditton P. *Law: The Old and New*. ANU Press, Canberra, 1980.

Berndt, C. H. and R. M. *Pioneers and Settlers*. Pitman Australia, Melbourne, 1978.

Berndt, C. H. and R. M. *The World of the First Australians*. Ure Smith, Sydney, 1964.

Berndt, R. M. *Love Songs of Arnhem Land*. Thomas Nelson, Melbourne, 1978.

Cole, K. *Aborigines of Arnhem Land*. Rigby, Sydney, 1979.

Coombs, H. C. *Kulinma*. ANU Press, Canberra, 1978.

Coombs, H. C., Dexter, B. G. and Hiatt L. R. 'The Outstation Movement in Australia', in the *Australian Institute of Aboriginal Studies* newsletter No. 14, p. 16, Canberra, 1980.

Elkin, A. P. *Aboriginal Men of High Degree*. Queensland University Press, Brisbane, 1977.

Elkin, A. P. *The Australian Aborigines*. Angus & Robertson, Sydney, 1974.

Gale, F. (ed). *Women's Role in Aboriginal Society*, Australian Institute of Aboriginal Studies, Canberra, 1974.

Groger-Wurm, H. M. *Australian Aboriginal Bark Painting in N.E. Arnhemland,* Australian Institute of Aboriginal Studies, Canberra, 1973.

Mountford, C. P. *Art, Myth and Symbolism of Australian Aborigines in Arnhem Land*. Melbourne University Press, Melbourne, 1956.

Robert, W. C. H. *The Dutch Explorers of Australia 1605–1756*. Philo Press, Amsterdam, 1973.

Roberts, J. *From Massacres to Mining*. CIMRA, London, 1978.

Rowley, C. D. *Outcasts in White Australia*. ANU Press, Canberra, 1971.

Rowley, C. D. *Remote Aborigines*. ANU Press, Canberra, 1971.

Rowley, C. D. *The Destruction of Aboriginal Society*. Penguin Books, Sydney, 1972.

Searcy, A. *In Northern Seas*. W. K. Thomas, Adelaide, 1905.

Shapiro, W. *Social Organisation in Aboriginal Australia*. ANU Press, Canberra, 1976.

Stone, S. (ed.) *Aborigines in White Australia*. Heinemann Educational Aust. Pty. Ltd., Melbourne, 1974.

Tatz, C. *Race Politics in Australia*. University of New England Publishing Unit, Armidale, 1979.

Warner, W. L. *A Black Civilisation*. Harper and Row, New York, 1958.